# The
# Professional

# The
# Professional

---

## Defining the
## New Standard
## of Excellence
## at Work

---

# Subroto Bagchi

Portfolio / Penguin

PORTFOLIO / PENGUIN
Published by the Penguin Group
Penguin Group (USA) Inc., 375 Hudson Street,
New York, New York 10014, U.S.A.
Penguin Group (Canada), 90 Eglinton Avenue East, Suite 700,
Toronto, Ontario, Canada M4P 2Y3
(a division of Pearson Penguin Canada Inc.)
Penguin Books Ltd, 80 Strand, London WC2R 0RL, England
Penguin Ireland, 25 St. Stephen's Green, Dublin 2, Ireland
(a division of Penguin Books Ltd)
Penguin Books Australia Ltd, 250 Camberwell Road, Camberwell,
Victoria 3124, Australia
(a division of Pearson Australia Group Pty Ltd)
Penguin Books India Pvt Ltd, 11 Community Centre, Panchsheel Park,
New Delhi – 110 017, India
Penguin Group (NZ), 67 Apollo Drive, Rosedale, Auckland 0632,
New Zealand (a division of Pearson New Zealand Ltd)
Penguin Books (South Africa) (Pty) Ltd, 24 Sturdee Avenue,
Rosebank, Johannesburg 2196, South Africa

Penguin Books Ltd, Registered Offices:
80 Strand, London WC2R 0RL, England

First American edition
Published in 2011 by Portfolio / Penguin,
a member of Penguin Group (USA) Inc.

1   3   5   7   9   10   8   6   4   2

Copyright © Subroto Bagchi, 2009
All rights reserved

LIBRARY OF CONGRESS CATALOGING IN PUBLICATION DATA

Bagchi, Subroto.
The professional : defining the new standard of excellence at work / Subroto Bagchi.
p. cm.
Includes index.
ISBN 978-1-59184-402-0
1. Professional employees. 2. Professional ethics. 3. Professions. I. Title.
HD8038.A1B34 2011
174'.4—dc22          2011001741

Printed in the United States of America
Set in Dante MT
Designed by Joy O'Meara

*To my daughters, Neha and Niti*

# Contents

# Contents

## Part Three   Professional Qualities

# Contents

# Contents

# The
# Professional

# Introduction

Some fifteen miles from central Philadelphia, at the northern edge of the city, stands the Cornwells Heights train station. It has a large parking lot, and on most weekdays, hundreds of commuters park their cars there before taking the twenty-minute train ride to Center City, the name the residents of the City of Brotherly Love have given to the downtown area.

Since the parking lot is some distance away from the platforms, the Southeastern Pennsylvania Transportation Authority (SEPTA), which operates Philadelphia's regional trains, runs a shuttle bus between the station and the parking lot. The drivers who operate these buses have an excruciatingly boring job. Hour after hour, they wait for the trains to arrive and then drive the passengers from the station to the parking lot, or the other way around, and then again wait for the next train. As they sit slumped in their seats, most drivers look as though they would do anything to escape the tedium. Curtis Perrin is an exception.

Perrin's demeanor and behavior reflect anything but boredom. Each time a passenger enters his bus, he calls out in his gritty, hearty voice: "Hey there, buddy! How are you today?" If an elderly woman enters, Curtis says, "Hello, young lady!" Even more remarkable than his wide smile and booming voice is his memory: Curtis remembers the cars that his passengers drive. While other drivers drive along a preassigned route—stopping at Parking Lots A, B, C, and so on, Curtis usually drives each passenger to his or her own car. As the exhausted passengers alight from the bus, he calls out again, "Have a great evening, buddy!" or "Happy Friday, sir. Have a great weekend." Curtis's way has endeared him to countless passengers; they sometimes bring him gifts when returning from their vacation. Some people bring him brownies and cakes on other occasions.

Curtis Perrin is an outstanding professional first and a bus driver second. His professionalism makes him view people as individual customers he serves and not as an anonymous mass of faceless commuters. On their part, people respond and react to Curtis's warmth; they don't see him as an invisible function but as someone with affective regard for his work. People like Perrin make a real difference to their work and to the people they serve. Curtis Perrin is a professional.

The word "profession" is defined by Merriam-Webster as "a calling requiring specialized knowledge and often long and intensive academic preparation." The same dictionary defines a "professional" as "participating for gain or livelihood in an activity or field of endeavor often engaged in by amateurs."

Although this is the standard definition, I have found throughout my career that the term "professional" often seems to imply different things to different people. As someone in the workforce, you probably have your own opinions about what makes a person a "professional." Perhaps you adhere strictly to Webster's definition and consider anyone who makes money doing what they do to be a professional—whether he or she is a plumber, a hedge fund manager, or a writer. Or maybe you have a stricter definition, one that requires people to be incredibly good at what they do in order to earn the label—a plumber who starts his own business, a hedge fund manager who earns millions by bringing in clients and managing their investments, a writer who has been published in every major newspaper or magazine in the country.

We also harbor notions about how professionals conduct themselves—they dress a certain way, avoid gossip, or refuse to discuss private matters with their colleagues unless it is relevant to their ability to do their job. Even in today's modern and relatively relaxed work environment, I often hear the term "professional" applied to people who adhere to these standards.

But after almost thirty-five years of life as a professional, I have found that, in the new era of the global economy, where every person's actions have the potential to have a global impact—whether good or bad—we must redefine what it means to be a true professional.

The word "professional" has been around for a long time, and its origins are even older. Its root dates back to A.D. 1175–1225 to the Latin word *professio*, which means an oath taken upon entering a religious order.

The reason we need to appreciate the origin of the term is that we live amid scores of qualified engineers, doctors, nurses, architects, lawyers, journalists, sportspersons and accountants who believe that being a professional is merely a means of earning a livelihood, just another way to get ahead in life, to seek and create further material comfort and eventually enjoy retirement. For such people, a professional is someone who gets an educational qualification to land a job, then a coveted assignment or posting, followed by a bunch of accelerated increments and promotions.

But in my view, a professional, especially now, is something more. Today, it's not enough for someone to just be able to do a job in order to qualify for this title; he or she not only must be able to accept responsibility for their own work and actions but also must understand how that work and those actions will translate to the rest of the world. Although every country, industry and company has its own code of conduct, there is no institution large enough or powerful enough to make sure each of us is behaving in the best way possible. Today, more than ever before, we must embrace the traditional meaning of the word "professional" and take a personal oath, promising we will do our best; we will bring our knowledge, skills and attitude to make a difference to others and to regulate ourselves.

And this does not just apply to "thought leaders" or men and women in suits. You could be a software engineer, a cosmetologist, an intellectual property lawyer or, for that matter, a publicist. For some of you—the doctors, lawyers and journalists, for instance—your profession has existed for a long time and therefore you probably already operate under a set of guidelines that has been long established. But for others, your profession may not have existed a hundred years ago. Every decade is throwing up brand-new professions the world over. On one hand, professionals in their respective fields are expected to be experts in their own disciplines, to understand their nuances and, at the same time, be able to work in tandem with their counterparts in other professions. But most important, they must be able to work across borders.

There has been an explosion in the world of professions, and yet there is still no system in place that can train people how to be true professionals. No matter how much education or training you have, there is no instruction manual that tells you how to approach every problem, communicate with different people and respond to change. As a result, most of us simply bumble our way into the critical, multifaceted understanding that separates a professionally qualified, technically competent individual from a handful of true professionals.

But there is another challenge to being a professional today. This is the fact that we work globally. Even those of us who don't travel for work often have to communicate with those halfway around the world and, of course, our reliance on international trade means we can easily be affected by an event that occurs or begins abroad.

Consider Ishani Mohapatra, who studied chemistry and specialized in nonedible flavoring agents. She completed college in Mumbai, India, but today works as a fragrance development manager at a company called International Flavors & Fragrances Inc. in Utrecht, the Netherlands. She works as part of a globally dispersed team that helps create new detergent fragrances for one of her company's clients, Procter & Gamble.

Or there's my chartered financial analyst, Leslie Davis, who advises me on international tax issues. Davis lives in California but has clients all over the world who turn to him on dual taxation issues in the course of their business with the United States.

In Bangalore, India, my dentist, Vivek Nandavar, is seeing an increase in the number of expatriate clients from many different countries as they make the Silicon Alley their place of work; of late he has also seen patients come from places like the Middle

East who are turning to India as a destination for affordable medical care, often combining it with tourism.

I have been working for the past thirty years as a professional. For fifteen of these years, I have been an entrepreneur. During this time, I have dealt with customers from all around the world. Even though I'm based in Bangalore, I wake up every morning to calls from Shanghai, London, California and other places far from home. I travel almost constantly and have lived overseas. I have raised venture capital money from investors across the world, and in 1999, I cofounded MindTree, which employs people from many different national origins and operates out of offices in the United States, Europe, Asia and Australia. Our nine thousand people create software applications for companies as diverse as John Wiley & Sons publishers in the United States and ArcelorMittal steel company in Europe. We develop and create technology that is used by companies from Denmark to Korea. Through my work in the software industry and through the work of my colleagues, I routinely transact with professionals from every discipline: technology folks, end users in finance and marketing and human resources, and sometimes medical doctors, lawyers, public relations experts and real estate agents.

In the same vein, as an individual who has traveled extensively and lived abroad several times, I have been a customer of a wide variety of professional services and have relied on countless experts from medical doctors to chiropractors to airline agents and auto repairers and cab drivers to help me solve a problem or accomplish a goal that I could not do alone. Each one is a professional whom we expect to satisfy our needs in a timely, cost-effective, inclusive, courteous and, of course, competent manner.

This book is as much about people like them as it is about those who readily come to mind when we think of the term "professional." It is as much for those who earn six-figure incomes as it is for those who earn minimum wage. In short, it is for everyone who recognizes the need to behave professionally.

What defines the true professional? My goal in this book is to answer this question.

I believe, at a fundamental level, there are three qualities that make someone a true professional. These are the ability to work unsupervised, the ability to certify the completion of a job or task and, finally, the ability to behave with integrity at all times.

But there are facets beyond meeting the base-level requirements. The true professional is also self-aware and is not afraid to admit when he or she is wrong, ask for help, or refuse to do something that does not align with his or her values or goals. He understands his limits but is never afraid to speak up when he feels silence can compromise an ethical boundary. He takes care of his body, soul, and mind and prioritizes everything he does in order to create maximum value.

The true professional has a long view of time. She understands that a profession is not limited to a particular job or organization but spans the entirety of her forty-plus-year career. She makes decisions and builds relationships knowing that the things she does today can affect her tomorrow, next week, next year or even ten years from now.

The true professional is one who evolves. He embraces the new challenges that each phase of his career brings and adapts to changes in his life, company, industry or culture. He excels not only at the technical details of his job but also at the managerial and leadership aspects that come with advancement.

The true professional is comfortable dealing with things she was not trained for. As we all know, we live in times when there is a high probability that an unlikely thing—from a natural disaster to a terrorist attack—could happen. The true professional sees these events not as catastrophes but as opportunities to make a difference.

Above all, the true professional understands the imperatives of our global economy. He is culturally aware, connected and engaged with people around the globe.

A final thought before we move on: I am not a management guru. I am a practitioner. My main profession is not writing books and lecturing at business schools but running my software business. Hence, I lay no claim to profound theories born of inscrutable research. I am an observer and a doer. For this reason my book shuns complexity, and for that matter sophistication. This is a simple book; it presents practical situations, ideas and concepts and exemplifies them with everyday lessons. It is not meant to be an academic pièce de résistance. It is a workbook for anyone who wants to excel in their careers, not only today, but decades from now. I would deem it worth your time if somewhere it makes you think, find your own "how to" and someday pass it on to others. Because I deeply believe it is simply not enough to be good at your work. A true professional must have a sense of legacy and leave the core of knowledge behind so that taller trees may one day sprout from the same ground into which we all must eventually fall.

Subroto Bagchi

Part One

# Integrity

# Chapter 1

# Burial of the Dead

Do you work in an entry-level position or even a middle-level job in a hotel, a hospital, a software company or a government organization? Or are you a self-employed professional like a doctor, a lawyer or a journalist? In all probability you are educated, know English and are working in (or have worked with) the corporate sector. Perhaps an MBA, or a student at an engineering college? You probably consider yourself a professional, or on the road to becoming one. Regardless of what you do or what stage of your career you're in, it's probably safe to say that your station in life is well above someone whose job is to, say, bury unclaimed corpses from city hospitals.

And yet this fact alone does not make you more of a professional. I know a man who has dedicated his life to dealing with dead bodies—unclaimed dead bodies. His job is dirty; it is morose; it requires no degree; yet he exhibits the true meaning of a professional more than most white-collar workers out there. His name is Mahadeva. He came to Bangalore as a child when one day his mother simply walked out on her entire village and her own family in a huff. Mother and son lived on the streets, and she worked to support him until the day she became sick. She brought herself and her son to the government-run Victoria Hospital. There she was admitted in a state of delirium, and her little son, Mahadeva, made the streets outside the hospital his home. He found many playmates among the urchins there and soon that world engulfed him. For the first time, little Mahadeva had people to play with—people who became his family—and he lost himself completely in this new world. Then one day someone told him his mother had died. Died? What was that? Where had he been when that happened?

The hospital had waited for someone to claim the dead body for the mandatory three days after death and, as often happens in countries like India where unclaimed dead bodies cannot be indefinitely kept at the morgue, had disposed of the body.

Now Mahadeva was an orphan.

A few people in the hospital ward raised money to help him go back to his village, but he refused to take it. That is when he met his benefactor, an old man who was a permanent fixture at the hospital. The man ran errands for poor, illiterate villagers who did not know the ways of the big city. He was the man who had secured a hospital bed for Mahadeva's mother. The old man took pity and asked Mahadeva to move in with him. Like Mahadeva, he did not have anyone in the world. Under his tutelage, Mahadeva grew up running errands in the hospital.

To Mahadeva, the hospital became the universe. One day, the police asked him to bury an unclaimed dead body and paid him two hundred rupees for the job. This was the day Mahadeva entered his profession, and he would go on to become the go-to guy for burying the city's unclaimed corpses. Every time the police picked up a dead body that had no claimants, Mahadeva was summoned. He had to do a turnkey job: pull the stiff body from the morgue, hire a horse-drawn carriage, put the body in it, take it to a burial ground and dig the grave all by himself—for only two hundred rupees. After completing the job, he would wait around in the hospital until he was summoned to do it all again.

Mahadeva did his work with such dedication, focus, care and concern that soon he was very much in demand. His workload increased and he bought his own horse-drawn carriage.

One day, the horse died.

People who had watched Mahadeva all these years came together and bought him an auto-rickshaw. Today, a picture of the horse has become Mahadeva's logo; it is painted on his rickshaw and appears on his business card. Mahadeva has buried more than 42,000 corpses in his lifetime, and his dedication has earned him phenomenal public recognition. Local gas stations do not charge him when his hearse is filled up, and the chief minister of Karnataka, the state in which Bangalore is located, thanked him for his selfless service to the abandoned citizens of Bangalore. Mahadeva is proud of his work, and today his son has joined him in the business.

Mahadeva: the high performer, and a true professional.

What are the two qualities Mahadeva has that make him a professional rather than someone who is simply professionally qualified?

One is his ability to work unsupervised, and the other is his ability to certify the completion of his work.

Whenever Mahadeva gets a call to go to the morgue, day or night, rain or shine, he arrives. His task is gruesome and difficult because there is usually no way to tell how or when someone died.

In his business, Mahadeva does not choose his clients. He accepts them in whatever size, shape or state they come. The day he buried the man who had taken him home after his mother died, he cried and bought the man a garland as a mark of his respect. That day, it occurred to him that he should be garlanding all the bodies he buried, not just that of his benefactor. Mahadeva believes that everyone—dead or alive—deserves respect no matter who they are or where they came from.

The police do not supervise Mahadeva, and he is not an employee of the hospital. He does not have a boss who writes his evaluation or gives him constructive feedback for continuous improvement. He reports to no one except himself. Whenever Mahadeva picks up a corpse, it goes straight to the burial ground—no place else. He completes the task with the immediacy it demands. And each time, he makes sure that all the steps are complete, from covering the dead body properly to digging six feet under, even though he knows no one is watching or would ever question him.

In most work environments, people who produce anything of economic value usually need supervision. A person who needs supervision is no professional. He is an amateur, maybe even an apprentice.

Ability to certify completion is an interesting and powerful idea. The concept is easy to understand when we look at the work of a painter, musician or sculptor. Who but only they can certify that their work is complete in all respects and is ready for the world? Who else but the painter knows that his painting did not need any more work, or that he could have done an even better job? How does the world know the musician or the sculptor truly did her best while creating something new for the world? Only they know.

That same ability to discern what constitutes completion and self-certify that the work is complete in all respects applies in equal measure to a software engineer who must write defect-free code, a young lawyer who is required to study a case and write a brief or a surgeon who must cut open a patient and make sure that he removes every instrument and every piece of gauze before stitching him up again.

# Chapter 2

# The Day Justice Was Murdered

On May 31, 2007, *The Times of India*, India's largest circulated newspaper, published a report that the Delhi police had sought the replacement of a public prosecutor by the name of I. U. Khan. Khan had been involved in a high-profile case in which a young man named Sanjeev Nanda had been tried for killing several people while driving drunk. The call for Khan's replacement followed a television exposé that showed how Khan had colluded with the defense attorney to bribe a crucial eyewitness in the case.

This story began in 1999 when Nanda, son of one of Delhi's high-flying families, drove a brand-new BMW through a police checkpoint and allegedly "mowed down" six people including three policemen. According to the prosecution, Nanda was traveling with his friends Manik Kapoor and Siddharth Gupta. After the fatal incident, Nanda stopped the car and got out to assess the damage. Then he got back into the car and drove off. Nanda then took the car to a friend's house and got it washed clean in an attempt to remove any evidence of the accident. A policeman, following the trail of dripping brake oil from the accident spot, came to the house and arrested the three young men. Later, in a highly publicized case, the defendants denied any involvement and maintained that the alleged driver was not at the scene and was not driving the car. Their lawyer, R. K. Anand, one of the top defense lawyers in the country, even presented theories that the accident was caused by a truck and not the BMW. Khan, the prosecutor, seemed to rest his case on the eyewitness account of a man named Sunil Kulkarni, who was at the scene of the crime. It was this man who was being sought to be bribed so that he would give false testimony. The transaction involving Khan, Anand and Kulkarni was caught on video and aired on prime-time television, causing huge public outrage.

Following this, Delhi police sought the permission of the High Court to replace Khan, and later the court found Khan and Anand guilty of obstructing justice. The High Court asked that they be barred from appearance in court for four months and that their title of senior advocate be removed. The matter went to the Supreme Court, which upheld the conviction of Anand but freed Khan from a contempt charge after reprimanding him for inappropriate conduct. Anyone with a basic sense of morality knows that bribing a witness is unethical, but what is even more shocking about this case is that the defense had help . . . from the *prosecution*!

My purpose in this chapter is not to recount a grisly story of wanton manslaughter by a drunken upper-class youth. Rather, my goal is to highlight professional ethics and the importance of displaying the highest standards of ethical behavior.

Here we are talking about two of India's top lawyers. One

of them has even represented two sitting prime ministers! The other's client list is equally impressive. These are not greenhorns in black coats. They went to law school; they were highly trained and had decades of experience to back them. How could they forget that, as representatives of the law, they could not try to unduly influence the course of justice? Did they not understand that, no matter how powerful they were, they could not compromise the interests of one of their clients?

Did Sanjeev Nanda murder those six men? The Indian Penal Code defines such killing, regardless of the number of victims, as culpable homicide not amounting to murder. Would he have done what he did if he had not been under the influence of alcohol? Probably not. A graduate of Wharton Business School at the University of Pennsylvania, Nanda had never done anything up until then that seemed to indicate he had the instincts of a killer. On the other hand, the two lawyers hired in the case did willfully attempt to kill justice. And in the process they defrocked themselves of the professional label.

Unlike Nanda, these men knew what they were doing; they cannot claim to have lost control of their basic senses due to inebriation. It was not a momentary indiscretion that made the defense lawyer conspire with the prosecutor. They knew they were breaching the professional code of ethics they'd been taught in law school. They did it in cold blood; it was a premeditated decision to buy off a star witness.

And it is not just the legal profession that should be bound by such tenets of professional conduct. The boundaries that these lawyers crossed apply in different ways to every profession.

What is professional ethical conduct and what actions may be deemed unprofessional?

What is the furthest boundary of ethics and integrity that, regardless of scrutiny and threat of punishment, every individual who calls himself a professional must think of, live by and live for? How can we learn to take responsibility for our actions and behave in the most professional way possible?

A young surgeon may not yet be proficient with the scalpel, but she must clearly understand what the basic tenets of medical practice are and what may constitute malpractice.

A software engineer, working on a client's project that requires complete confidentiality, cannot discuss his work with people not preapproved by the client (and that includes his spouse, or a significant other, or a friend at a pub). He cannot brag about his work to others because it may compromise the confidentiality requirements of a customer with his organization.

A journalist cannot curry favor with a source to get a scoop or use professional standing to seek special accommodations from the system.

A chief executive of a company cannot appoint his spouse as a contractor in his own office and do business with her.

A boss who is lending a sympathetic ear to an emotionally distressed employee cannot use her situational fragility to take her to bed.

A policeman cannot prey on a citizen who has come to seek help.

Every profession has some explicit and some implicit code of conduct, and understanding that serves as the distinction between a professionally qualified person and a professional.

Beyond the capacity to work without the need for supervision and the ability to deduce what may constitute completion of work, anyone who seeks entry into the club of professionals must understand integrity and must practice it every step of the way. Without integrity, any professionally qualified individual is actually a danger to society.

# Chapter 3

# Integrity Is Personal

My first few lessons in professional integrity came from my father, who was a small-time public servant in India's eastern state of Orissa. He drove home the fundamental tenet that resources provided to you to discharge your official duty do not belong to you. It started with using—or rather not using—his office staff and his official jeep for personal needs. It was, and is, customary for officers to use people employed by the government as household help. But not my father. The first time he was given a jeep by the government, it was garaged at the government housing allotted to him. I have never seen my mother in it. We could sneak in to sit in the jeep only when it was stationary and my father was not anywhere in the neighborhood. He was the district employment officer, but he would not even drive to work in the jeep. He chose to walk instead because he believed that the vehicle belonged to the republic, not him, and that it was only meant to be used on his tours to the interiors of the tribal district of Koraput where he was posted.

We studied in run-down government schools and, occasionally, some of our friends used to bring paper and other stationery to school that their parents had brought home from their offices. In small-town India, this was no big deal. But any conversation about the subject would upset my father. Not only did he have a strong opinion on such things, he did not like us to bring home gossip on the subject.

After my father retired from government work, we moved in with my brother, who had by then joined the Indian Administrative Service (IAS). As a trainee, he was starting his career as a subdivisional officer, responsible for overseeing the law and order as well as development of part of a larger district. The state provided him an official residence as was the norm for such functionaries. In case of my brother, it was a bungalow with a large compound on which nothing grew. The land was lying unused. One day, I proposed to my mother that we plow the land and grow some lentils. I suggested we get a tractor from a family friend, and my mother seemed sympathetic to the idea. So one day, lo and behold, the tractor arrived at the gate. I perched on it excitedly and oversaw the plowing operation. The next step would have been sowing the lentil seeds. But that was not to be.

When my father returned home, he was shocked to see what was going on and he admonished me, giving me a long lecture on landownership and the meaning of land use. While it was okay to tend a small kitchen garden in the house allotted to a government servant, one could not push the envelope and start cultivating on government land. That day, I also received a tutorial on the meaning of the word "encroachment" as defined by the Orissa Revenue Act of 1951, which he read to me. I was just twelve years old at the time, but I got the message for the rest of my life.

A part of the large bunglow was designated as the residential office of the subdivisional officer. In it, there was a big wooden table where mounds of files were stacked each night for my brother to go through and that were replaced the next day. On the table, next to the files, sat a black phone. It was the first time in our lives that my family had seen a telephone at home. For someone like me who was born in a house with no running water or electricity, the telephone was an object of curiosity and pride.

When it rang, it sent electrifying energy through my entire being. I wanted to pick up the phone to answer it whenever my brother was not around. It felt so grown up. My father maintained a hawkeye on the instrument and prohibited me from even touching it. Forget about talking to friends (most did not have a phone anyway); going near it was forbidden because it belonged to the republic.

Those early lessons made it easy for me to understand later on the demarcation between what belongs to Caesar and what belongs to me. I never needed a formal course on corporate governance.

Sometimes, Father's ways seemed strange and extreme. But I realized how relevant his messages were when, back in 1990, I was the resident manager for U.S. operations for Wipro. One day, my most important customer called. He was extremely embarrassed about the subject of conversation, but at the same time wanted me to know that one of our engineers was making personal long-distance calls to Chennai, India, using the telephone in the office in Austin, Texas. He had run up close to a thousand dollars in making those surreptitious phone calls. Until then, the client did not have pass code protection on telephones and every phone in the office was equipped with long-distance calling capability so the U.S. team could be in constant touch with their counterparts in Japan. My head hung in shame at my colleague's breach of integrity. It was not generational poverty that had led the engineer to make personal phone calls from the office telephone; it was lack of basic understanding of what did not rightfully belong to him.

Over the years, working in India and overseas, I have learned to correlate professional integrity and good business, taking off from where my father's grounding ended. Today, I can say with absolute certainty that integrity in business and work is not a matter of corporate piety—it simply makes good business sense. Globally, positive examples abound in every sphere. But more about that later. Let us first understand what integrity means in the professional context.

Simply said, it means:

- We follow the rules.
- Where rules do not exist, we use fair judgment.
- When in doubt, we do not go ahead and do what suits us; we seek counsel.
- Finally, faced with a difficult choice, we ask ourselves: Can my act stand public scrutiny without causing embarrassment to me and my family?

If these four tenets are applied to our daily decisions, answers to the most daunting questions will present themselves and our subsequent professional conduct will always meet the highest standards of integrity.

In civil societies, all professions are bound by rules that usually have a basis in fairness. Sometimes, the rules do not suit the professional or business interests of an individual in a given transaction. The thing to do then is not to bend or circumvent or flout the rule that does not suit you, but to contest it and, pending resolution, follow it. This is what constitutes the basic obligation of any professional. So when a tax law does not suit me, I will protest the law, but while protesting it, I must ensure that my business pays the tax (albeit under protest) until such time as that law or its interpretation has been reversed by the system. I cannot be part of a system and flout the law at the same time. If I live in a country, my citizenship requires me to embrace the legal system in its entirety. The moment we selectively subscribe to the legal system, it will fail.

No society can, however, fully state all the norms of acceptable professional behavior through enacted laws. No corporation can tell you exactly what, as professionals, you should or should not be doing. This is why we need to use fair judgment. In fact, if we exercise fair judgment most of the time, one does not require a framework of rules.

The concept of fair judgment is subjective, but essentially it is the voice of conscience. The basic question you need to ask yourself is: How would I feel if someone did to me what I am about to do to another?

So here I am, planning to take a shortcut and bend the rules against the system. All I need to do is step back for just one moment and ask, What if I were the system? What if I were at the receiving end of things? When a moment of temptation comes, as it sometimes must, all we need to do is switch roles and place ourselves in the shoes of the potentially most-affected party. In an instant, the path presents itself.

Most problematic professional situations can be avoided if,

before committing to a certain path, a professional just picks up the phone and asks someone he trusts and respects what to do. Seeking counsel is an almost certain way of preventing problematic situations from arising in the very first place and then becoming a matter of perpetual regret.

Finally, the greatest deterrent for most of us is public scrutiny. Even if we have our moments of private indiscretion, there are only certain things we are comfortable with sharing publicly. If we simulate the possibility that what we are about to do might be uncovered, the choice will become clear. How would I truly feel in front of my family if my indiscretion was scrutinized or came to light? That one thought is enough to show me the path in most situations where I may be drawn toward the convenient, but not the right thing to do.

# Chapter 4

# Doctor, Heal Thyself

On February 9, 2008, *The Guardian* newspaper in London ran a report about an Indian doctor who had fled to Nepal after being investigated for his alleged complicity in running an illegal kidney racket.

Amit Kumar was accused of running a private hospital just outside Delhi that allegedly lured or forced hundreds of poor people into "donating" their kidneys. Kumar then sold the organs and made a fortune.

He was arrested in a resort very close to the Indian border. At the time of the arrest he had a bank draft for 900,000 rupees and cash piles of 140,000 euros and 20,000 dollars Kumar apparently kept a low profile in the hotel where he was staying, wearing a hat and sunglasses, but aroused suspicion when it was found that he was cutting stories about the kidney scam from newspapers. According to the police, he was attempting to flee to Canada where he owned a home. On his arrest, Kumar addressed the press, insisting that he had not committed any crime, that he was not running away and was confident he would be cleared. Investigators, however, said he had confessed to carrying out the illegal kidney harvests. He and his brother had run the racket together, selling the organs to American, Greek and British nationals.

We presume that Amit Kumar had taken the Hippocratic oath as a medical graduate before entering the profession. Irrespective of every other test of integrity, all he had to do was to ask four simple questions before doing what he did:

- Is my intended act consistent with the law of the land?
- Is what I am going to do the fair thing?
- If I were to seek counsel from someone with no vested interest, would the person advise me that it was the right thing to do?
- Would it embarrass me if the news of what I intend to do broke out?

Amit Kumar, also known as Dr. Santosh Raut, ran the racket in Mumbai and Delhi and was prosecuted in Mumbai, from where he had jumped bail. In Mumbai he conned beggars and street dwellers into selling their organs. In Mumbai and Delhi he had a network of nurses who were paid large amounts of money to get the victims to his operating room.

Doctors and nurses are professionally qualified people. But when they breach the principles of integrity, they cease to be professionals. When such people are faced with a conflict and they are about to breach the principles of professional integrity, it is not always the law but fair judgment that can prevent them from crossing the line.

Breach of integrity is not relevant for doctors and nurses alone. It is a virus that infects every profession. On April 20, 2004, a top editor at *USA Today*, Karen Jurgensen, abruptly resigned her position at the newspaper for her failure to intercept a series of fabricated stories by foreign correspondent Jack Kelley. Kelley had fabricated substantial portions of eight major articles, including one that was a Pulitzer finalist (an eyewitness account of a suicide bomber that turned out to be nothing more than a figment of Kelley's imagination).

From Amit Kumar to Jack Kelley, most of the people you will read about in this book were educated, well informed and mostly affluent. They had a choice at every step and they chose to do what was convenient, not what was right.

At the end of the day, professionalism is a personal choice people make, and for some, integrity simply becomes a way of life.


In many parts of the developing world, young people do not work part time while studying in high school or college. In contrast, in many Western countries such a thing is more the norm. While working part time as gas station attendants, grocery packers or baristas in a coffee shop, young people begin to understand the boundaries of a professional work environment. Most of them begin to appreciate the concept of company time versus personal time, the idea of serving a paying customer, acceptable workplace behavior and the difference between the penny in their pockets and that in the cash register.

Further, in many places around the world, the education system fails to provide an understanding of the idea of professionalism. There is little content on the concept of professional ethics in technical or professional curricula. And there is no conversation about the subject. In the absence of all that grounding, despite being professionally educated, most young people come into the workplace as novices.

Finally, most workplaces do not articulate their position; far fewer practice ethical behavior in any demonstrable manner. This is not to imply that they do not abide by the law. What I am saying is that most fail to consciously articulate a shared understanding of ethical behavior, what it actually means in that particular work environment and how it should be practiced by everyone at work. And in only a very few companies is ethical behavior truly nonnegotiable.

Chapter 5

# The Many Shades of Gray

While there is only one pope at the head of the Roman Catholic Church, in the Hindu world, religious leadership is quite decentralized and there are many who are considered to be religious heads. Prominent among them are the *shankaracharyas*. Unlike the pope, who sits in Rome, these shankaracharyas have their seats in different places of religious significance. One such sits in the southern Indian temple town of Kanchi, famous for its ancient architectural beauty and fine handloom cloth. On December 18, 2008, a report filed by the India Abroad News Service (IANS) sent shockwaves throughout the Hindu world. It reported that charges were pressed against the shankaracharya of Kanchi along with his successor; the charges involved murder and financial embezzlement. As the story unfolded in the following weeks, there were allegations and media reports about sexual wrongdoing in Kanchi's religious high place as well.

The world over, stories like these involving the heads of religious orders have made news in recent times. These often make us question morality itself. The conduct of individuals like these rubs off on the institutions they represent. Their personal conduct becomes synonymous with institutional conduct. In difficult times like ours, we all look up to individuals beyond ourselves for reassurance, to get clarification on what to do when we are at a crossroads.

When we are children and things around us fail, we look to our parents for value clarification. Later in life, we look up to a teacher or a mentor. Beyond them all, we seek regulation and protection from the idea of the government, which to most of us is the protector of civil society, the arbiter of laws and norms that dictate how all citizens must behave. But beyond the government, we turn to our religious leaders—a parish priest, a shankaracharya, an imam or a rabbi.

In the last couple of decades, we have seen this established model break down with dismaying regularity.

In the United States, we saw an elected president compromise the sanctity of his office by giving in to the allure of sex; we saw him lie under oath. We saw big business—from New York Stock Exchange chairman Richard Grasso to Martha Stewart to the folks at Enron to Satyam Computers chairman Ramalinga Raju—fail the test of transparency. The successive convulsions in the U.S. Catholic church involving serious accusations of sexual abuse left people wondering: Where is our source of strength in times of difficulty? Who clarifies values?

To me, large institutions in particular have progressively exposed their own vulnerability. When obviously unethical things happen in places we hold in high regard, people begin to discount the subsequent messages they receive from them. It works like this: If a child witnesses a parent giving or taking a bribe or listens to parental conversations that validate such things, the child will actually begin to associate these despicable acts with those she looks up to. When the same child listens to lectures in school about the importance of being truthful or not taking what does not belong to her, she will not actually "hear" the message because she has already witnessed people she trusts disobeying it. If it's all right for them to ignore this advice, why shouldn't she?

One day, the same child, now grown up and professionally qualified, joins the workplace, already a cynic about the benefits of integrity, and will discount her organization's values. This creates significant challenges for business organizations that value integrity and expect their people to be principled in their personal and professional capacities. But how do you communicate a code of conduct to someone who is a witness to the positional collapse of values at home, in the government, in big business and in organized religion?

Posters, screen savers and first-day orientations at work during which we hear corporate rah-rah by folks from the human resource department do not work anymore. The only option left for those in positions of leadership is to talk the talk and walk the walk. They need to be transparent and explain to others what transparency means and why it is good for everyone.

While leaders need to demonstrate high personal integrity in order to deliver the message to their organizations, the truth is that value clarification is most needed not when things are going right but during dark moments, when things are falling apart. People do not appreciate values when everything is going well.

Each time there is a fiscal irregularity, or a report of misuse of power, or sexual misconduct at the workplace, we invariably get caught up in two things: First, facts and emotions get mixed up. Then, we get lost in what is called the "many shades of gray." This is the moment of truth.

People falter when they begin looking at professional misconduct not in black and white but in shades of gray. Once you let yourself enter the gray zone, you get lost, because the human eye can actually see 108 shades of gray! Once you become mired in the many shades of gray, value clarification takes a backseat, for the majority of people find taking a black-and-white stand on a breach of integrity an uncomfortable proposition. Some managers skirt the determination of facts and let emotions cloud their judgment. They get cold feet dealing with a breach of ethical conduct because they do not like to be in the position of a hangman.

The other fear people have is about organizational embarrassment and business loss. Consider the following situation.

You have just discovered that your star salesperson has faked a travel voucher. He is negotiating a huge order. The discovery has taken place at a time when he is about to close this very valuable deal, which will make the company a lot of money. And he is the only person who knows the ropes in the client organization.

What would you do?

- Keep quiet?
- Warn him and let it go?
- Warn him only after the order comes in?
- Fire him on the spot?

Think.

# Chapter 6

# Firing the Star Salesperson

We left our story as you were deciding what to do with the star salesperson who had forged a travel voucher. The path you choose affects the organization.

I cannot tell you what you should be doing. It really depends on your personal and organizational value system, and I certainly hope the two are not opposed to each other. On this issue, rather than give you a prescriptive outcome, let us talk about the process organizations must have in place in order to deal with breaches of integrity.

First of all, an organization needs to articulate its position on integrity. As a part of that articulation, it needs to publish the process for dealing with how a breach is reported. The organization needs to anticipate potential breaches; even in the most well meaning of places, sometimes things will go wrong. The process for dealing with a breach should consider: Who can report the breach? Who will investigate it? What steps should be followed during the investigation? The consequences of a breach of integrity must be common knowledge. At MindTree, for instance, we have articulated an integrity policy. This is not left in the wilderness of the intranet portal. It is freely downloadable from our Web site. We keep the document current with instances of breaches as they sometimes take place and the price the organization paid each time. There is a whistle-blowing process, and when a breach is reported, we set up something akin to prosecution and defense teams so that facts and emotions are separated and witch-hunting does not take place. We investigate issues without fear or favor and irrespective of who is involved and what the business implications could be.

Assuming that an organization is committed to an in-depth investigation of the reported breach, the most important area where many flounder is speed. More than anything else, speed is critical. You do not want to drag your feet because the matter is embarrassing or the potential outcome is inconvenient. The greater the delay, the greater the chance of people moving from black and white to the many shades of gray. That is what happens under the judicial system in most cases of public investigation. An organization must not fall into the same trap.

If the issue of complicity is factually settled as a result of the investigation, the organization must brace itself to absorb the consequences. If you know that a salesperson has forged a bill, and such forgery is defined as a breach of integrity by the organization, at that moment it matters very little that his firing could adversely affect the outcome of a bid in progress or subsequently affect employee morale. This is the classic moment of truth. It is true that the action of management could mean loss of business, but the clarity with which management thinks and the speed with which it acts determine the consequent social memory that guides the vast majority of employees and eventually makes organizational values tangible.

The most critical aspect of dealing with issues of integrity is the price management is willing to pay to ensure integrity in the workplace. Once people figure that out, compliance does not require constant policing.

Following definitive action, the next step is communication. This is not always easy. A senior vice president is being asked to leave on charges of sexual harassment. Would you or would you not explain the circumstances to his direct reports? What acts must be publicly and widely communicated and what acts require that the individual concerned be given a safe passage? Do not focus on getting the "right answers" to these questions. The bigger question is whether or not an organization encourages conversation and has an existing framework to deal with such issues.

Finally, all is not over just because you have decided to part ways with a delinquent colleague. It is not just a matter of firing someone. The organization needs to deal with the inevitable—the residual toxicity of such incidents. The responsibility of management does not end with handling a breach with speed and fairness; it must be very sensitive to the emotional fallouts that such acts leave behind. When a breach is dealt with, top management has to help the organization in making sense of the situation and the subsequent decision. It has to shift from blame to building collective learning for the future. It must identify individuals and groups who may need help to heal. After all, the fired salesperson could also be a much-loved colleague of many years and the senior vice president may have been a great problem solver and a role model in other ways for people below him.

Apart from such people, the process invariably affects those who have investigated the issue or corroborated facts that lead to someone getting fired. These individuals tend to develop what I call "hangman's remorse." It is important to keep communication channels open and encourage such people to talk even after the event is over. This helps to reinforce the idea that their action was not just something required as part of their job but was indeed the right thing to do.

Having done all of this, an organization should know that residual toxicity could remain within the larger organization among those not close to the incident. This can occur when a silent majority forms its own opinion and does not express it but lets it fester. Positive reinforcement, visible actions of top management and constancy of purpose are needed to detoxify the silent majority. And be prepared—the actual healing takes a long time.

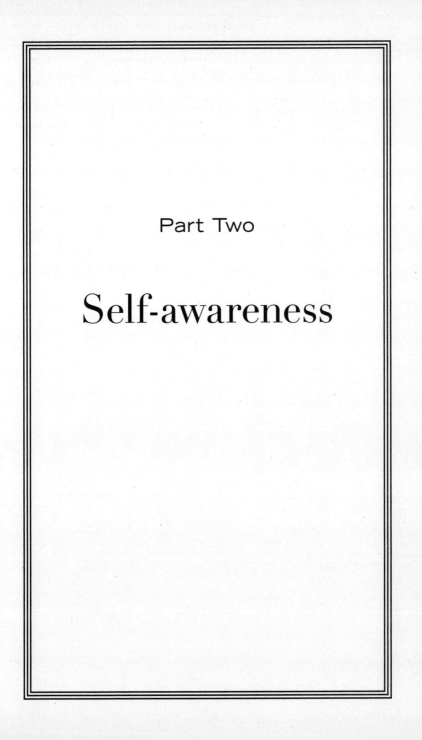

Part Two

# Self-awareness

# Chapter 7

# Where Competence Ends

Two African American men. Both born in the same decade—one in 1943, the other in 1947. Both sports stars of formidable fame. Raised by ordinary parents, both were endowed with enormous talent, and won prestigious college scholarships to pursue their game. Both worked hard, extremely hard, to reach the highest level of their professions. Both achieved prestige, acclaim and fame.

But behind the glamour, there was pain. In time, both men had their own brushes with the law. One for crimes ranging from shoplifting to murder. The other for protesting apartheid and oppression against immigrants from Haiti.

One went to the hall of notoriety and the other to the hall of fame. The former is American football player O. J. Simpson and the latter was the tennis legend Arthur Ashe.

Both had unmatched professional skills, but Simpson can never be regarded as a true professional. Ashe, a man who died of an HIV infection he received via a blood transfusion after a heart attack, lives on in the hearts of millions of people around the world who have little to do with professional tennis.

In the grueling world of professional sports where only the best survive, it takes something more than the highest batting average, the most formidable backhand, or the most MVP awards to be a professional. What separates O. J. Simpson and Arthur Ashe is self-awareness—this is the streak that divides millions of professionally qualified people in multiple disciplines from the few hundreds who inspire professional respect.

Some people are naturally more self-aware than others. But all of us have the capacity to become progressively self-aware through life's experiences. Without self-awareness, we fail to balance ourselves through the ups and downs of life, have problems in accepting reality and often do not know what is good for us. As a result, we may even end up making wrong professional choices that have a spiraling downward impact.

What constitutes self-awareness? How do we build self-awareness? What signs indicate the evolution of this idea in our journey to becoming a true professional?

In this section, I discuss some critical qualities of self-aware people. These qualities, I believe, build on the foundation of integrity and ethics, and will take you along the path of developing into a true professional in your chosen sphere of work.

Chapter 8

# Knowing Who You Are

---

It is important that each one of us pushes our limits and operates outside our known boundaries so that we explore new possibilities. Yet it is also important not to get carried away—particularly at the height of one's career. In societies where a certain degree of sycophancy is part of the accepted code, it is easy for one to reach too far. A famous actor who is able to portray varied characters with great conviction on the silver screen begins to believe that in real life he could do as good a job, becomes a member of Parliament and then falls flat. It is one thing to play the role of a leader of people on film; it is quite another to execute that in real life. Examples abound in every other field.

Always remain aware of where you have come from and where you are today. Being grounded is a key requirement for carrying success on your shoulders without being burdened by it. I come across many professionals who shun their roots, because it brings on a sense of personal inadequacy. Sometimes they prefer to adorn their conversations with false accents, carefully donning clothes that they hope cover up the anonymity of their early upbringing. Many cling to the branding acquired through a degree or diploma of a certain institution.

Do not let yourself get carried away; do not start believing in the myth about yourself and your achievements. The self-aware understand what their true strengths are; they know exactly how much of their success is because of their inherent strengths and how much is situational. Many of us are extremely fortunate to have been mentored by the right people, fortunate to be in positions of great influence sometimes through sheer luck, or have been the children of fortuitous circumstance where we were surrounded with very competent people who did not compete for credit. None of these take away from our success. Believing that any consequent success is only due to one's inherent capacity is dangerously wrong. Once we begin to think and believe this, we have reached the beginning of the end. We lose our bearings at great cost. Once lost, it often takes a terrible personal loss to restore sanity. Showered with undeserved adulation and recognition, self-aware professionals remind themselves and others around them that their personal qualifications and abilities have only brought them so far. And they take both success and failure with the same equanimity.

# Chapter 9

# Being Authentic

The phone rings. The caller is someone I've known only as a casual acquaintance at best. I have not heard from him in a decade.

"How've you been? I've been reading so much about you and the success of your company. I really admire what you've achieved. I have read your blog," he gushes. "By the way, my uncle was asking about you the other day. He thinks very highly of you." The caller's uncle was a person of eminence, but I had had one brief meeting with him many years ago, and I doubted he would be inquiring about me through his nephew.

There's honey dripping from the caller's voice; I'm beginning to feel uncomfortable with all the praise and familiarity. Where is the conversation leading? I wonder.

And then comes the real purpose. The caller is looking to change jobs. "I manage a $400 million account, you know," he says. I'm wary when people make such claims. "Managing an account" usually means the person stopped doing real work a while ago. Even though MindTree did not have much interest in the domain he worked in, I asked him to send in his CV, offering to put him in touch with the head of a division who could possibly use his services.

A couple of days later I received the CV and forwarded it to my colleague. Imagine my surprise when I discovered that my so-called admirer had already been in touch with my colleague and had sent his CV even before calling me. Now why did he conveniently forget to mention this to me? The story does not end here.

A few days later, I was having lunch with a friend who is the CEO of a firm in the same sector. He casually said, "Your protégé has been in touch with us. Tell me, is he really good? He told us, if we wanted to know more about his work, we only had to ask you."

"Whom are you talking about? I haven't recommended anyone to you."

No surprises here: my "protégé" was the out-of-the-blue caller. He had gone ahead and offered my name as a reference without even asking me first!

There is no point in being inauthentic and insincere. A true professional has no need to embellish, name-drop, or pretend to be something he's not. Being authentic might not always get us what we want, but that is better than the ignominy of being unmasked, because we live in a small world where everything is connected, and the hollowness of our sincerity will eventually be revealed.

The professional world really craves authenticity; do not dismiss it as old-fashioned.

# Chapter 10

# Being Comfortable

As we advance in our careers, we outgrow many inadequacies of our past. We gain through the experience of the assignments we handle; we acquire fresh knowledge from others that equips us to handle things differently from the past. Yet the self-aware professional is conscious that there is bound to be some gap in his knowledge, knows that he may never bridge this gap and, most important, feels comfortable with this fact.

A long time ago, I met a customer who, while saying good-bye to me at the end of a long and happy association, told me that I should be comfortable about not being technically qualified, even though I was working in the R&D section of an IT company. During my time there, I used to attend myriad meetings with our customers and engineers and must have shown some fallibility somewhere that did not escape the customer's attention. He was giving me advice on the importance of developing comfort with personal inadequacies. After that I have never felt uneasy about being a graduate in political science working in the IT industry. More important, I do not pretend to understand things when I cannot.

Today, I work for MindTree, where highly competent teams tackle complex technical problems. However capable I might be, I simply cannot fathom the complexity and depth of their work. I may sometimes be capable of deep questioning, I may have the intuitive capacity to cut through issues, I may have the breadth of experience to bring in an external viewpoint which blinkered teams that work at the cutting edge of technology may miss—yet none of that gives me the ability or competence to write a software algorithm or understand the physics of how the alternating character of material helps us store information in bits and bytes.

I may add value in some meetings, and not in others. When technical experts speak, my silence may signal my total lack of understanding. But if I open my mouth, I may disturb the harmony. A professional does not need to hog the limelight or monopolize airtime.

If you cannot add true value, then you must not add to the problem by pretending. The more you pretend, the more naked you become. Ever since I received this piece of momentous advice from a guardian angel, I have attended countless meetings where I began by admitting that I am a complete novice or have sat quietly while others have taken center stage, and I have never felt excluded or reduced in stature because of it.

Sometimes, stating your ignorance can be the simplest solution. Others then take it upon themselves to explain complex technical jargon in easy-to-understand language. Concede the ground and wait, emotionally secure. The team will come back to you when they need you, and then you can truly add value.

# Chapter 11

# Seeking Help

Each one of us may have the education and training that make us competent at our jobs. These are our strengths, and we must build on them.

But as I mentioned earlier, there is always bound to be a gap in our training and knowledge to do all the things our jobs may entail, and in such situations, admitting ignorance is just one step. Actively seeking to bridge that gap is the next important step in becoming self-aware. Quite often, it is achieved by seeking help from others.

Seeking help from someone—a peer, a mentor, your supervisor, even a junior—is not a sign of weakness. We are surrounded by knowledgeable people in our own organizations and certainly outside of them. But we feel self-conscious about actively seeking their help. We are plagued with self-doubt: What if a peer uses the context to showcase himself as better than me? What if my junior loses respect for me if I ask for help? Am I exposing diminished capacity or intellect by admitting I need help?

These can be real risks sometimes. But again, if a professional does not take risks, how will he develop emotional self-confidence? The moment we seek help, we actually expand inner capacity; we create the emptiness into which others pour their capabilities.

Seeking help is not always about solving an organizational problem. Sometimes we may have a personal problem—an emotional issue, an awkward health matter—which we keep to ourselves. Sooner rather than later, it will adversely affect our work.

There is no shame in asking for help—in matters of work or in matters of mental and physical well-being.

Chapter 12

# Not Suffering False Comparisons

Every professionally qualified person makes comparisons with colleagues, peers, seniors, even juniors some time or other. Such comparisons arise because of a competitive spirit that is built into us, often through a ruthless social and educational system that teaches us to falsely interpret the meaning of success in material terms.

Every now and then I meet people who constantly compare themselves with those whom they have left behind decades ago, sometimes pegging their measure of success on where former colleagues or classmates might be today.

Consider this. A midcareer doctor who has embraced the life of research is constantly nagged by the so-called material success of a colleague who was a comparatively mediocre medical student but is now minting money because he chose to open a private practice fifteen years ago. Our man loses faith in his own work and achievements, regretting the years he has lost, unable to turn the clock back. Falsely attracted to the other person's station in life, he yearns for the other man's money, not realizing that the individual in question may be leading a less than complete life. Quite possibly he has no time to enjoy his money! But no tertiary consideration yields solace. The shadow of comparison progressively engulfs the researcher so that eventually he loses focus, gets pulled in by a chimera and sacrifices that most precious thing: contentment.

It is futile to make such comparisons. They cause unnecessary pain, based as they usually are on superficial knowledge, and are certainly devoid of an understanding of the other person's journey to reach that position.

Chapter 13

# Having a Reasonable
# View of the Future

Do we all know with certainty where we are headed?

Probably not. Yet when you look around and observe the professionals you admire in various fields, you invariably sense that they seem to know where they are going; they are in command of the situation even as they face the indeterminate challenges of the future. This comes from the ability to build a view of the future, as against being helplessly dragged into it by unknown forces.

Building a view of the future, and knowing where you are headed, requires acknowledgment of the ground reality, a statement of intent in the overall direction, and sometimes a clear destination or purpose. The sense of destination gives people what celebrated psychologist and author Viktor Frankl calls "something to look forward to" in his book *Man's Search for Meaning*. The author survived the Holocaust at the notorious Auschwitz concentration camp and others in Germany during the Second World War. This is where he studied the psychology of people who survived the worst brutality and hopelessness anyone could ever experience. Yet those who survived the concentration camp did so on the strength of their sense of journey.

They believed that they would get out of the place some day.

They believed that they had an unfinished task to do.

In that belief, they felt that it was they who were in charge despite the helpless immediacy of their circumstances.

# Chapter 14

# Looking Beyond Money

A professional who sees his work primarily as a means of earning money runs out of meaning very soon. After you've achieved basic comforts, the quest for material success actually erodes self-worth. It becomes most pronounced in the later part of one's life. Many among us begin to suffer from a sense of emptiness that becomes difficult to decode. The greatest satisfaction, and the more enduring one for a professional, is the admiration of people with whom we do business. At a certain stage in one's career, it is peer recognition that sustains us. But beyond it all, the ones who last the longest in the race are those who have given something back to their professions. These are professionals who are driven by a sense of legacy. There is no sustenance bigger than the power to build an intellectual and emotional inheritance.

Many midcareer professionals nurse an empty desire to do something beneficial for a larger common good. "I want to make a difference to society" is often just false piety. Do small things on a sustained basis; do things for your own profession; do things that make a difference to you, your family, your friends, your neighbors and your colleagues; do not worry about changing the world.

The day you feel empty, shift the attention from yourself to others—go and spend time with a bunch of colleagues who have just joined the organization, help an intern with her work, write a series of how-to articles based on your experiences, take on pro-bono work with your industry association. See how the pitcher of emptiness begins to fill again.

## Chapter 15

# Being Deeply Self-observant

During leadership training sessions, I often ask groups of people to close their eyes for a few minutes in a quiet place and count the number of sounds they can identify. It is a very interesting exercise. Participants usually pick up the rustle of paper, footsteps, the sound of a distant automobile, a chair softly creaking as someone shifts position, probably a conversation in the corridor, the ping of an incoming message on someone's BlackBerry.

When the exercise ends and people recount what they have heard, most people invariably miss two things: sometimes the soft hum through the air-conditioning duct, and almost inevitably the sound of their own breathing. When you can hear your own breathing, you are beginning to observe yourself. But this is just the surface of self-observation. Just as you can observe your body, you can learn to observe your own mind.

Learning to be self-observant is learning how to watch yourself as you think, as you work and interact with others.

I learned to be self-observant in my professional life when I was a rookie salesman. As I went from sales call to sales call, I learned not only to make the call but to observe what was happening. From the time I opened the customer's door, I observed the way we greeted each other, the smallest details of the office, how we settled down, how I initiated the conversation, the questions I was asked and the answers I gave, the tiniest reaction of rejection, query or approval, how the conversation flowed, and how we finally concluded.

The capacity to watch your own actions and utterances is the starting point of being self-observant. This can take you to a state where you can observe thoughts, feelings and actions. For example, if I cannot see myself when I become angry, if I do not play back such a moment, frame by frame, I will never be able to identify whether the cause, the degree of my reaction and its effect was appropriate, adequate or over the top and unacceptable.

Being self-observant is an amazing way to help you perform an "action replay" each time. Record events—who said what, who did what and how things unfolded—and play them back later. Watch yourself at work; you will be amazed how much you will learn about yourself, and this will help you move forward. In the process, you become both player and coach.

Observing yourself on a daily basis and replaying your actions and reactions does not mean you cease to be natural, or lose spontaneity. Just as the player on the sports field is unconcerned with the camera recording the game, the professional is able to go with the flow, be natural and normal, but has the capacity to record events and faithfully reconstruct them down to the smallest detail. The camera is in the mind. Self-observant people do not suffer from illusions.

# Chapter 16

# Reining in Reactions

Once, I was talking with a bellboy at the Taj Coromandel Hotel in Chennai. He had worked in the same hotel all his life. During our conversation, I asked him what was the worst situation he had ever faced in his job in all the years he had worked there.

After a long silence, the man recounted an irate guest who, for no reason, had flung a bag at him as they were going up in the elevator.

"What did you do when he did that?" I asked.

"Nothing, sir. I felt very bad. Then I thought something had probably made the guest angry." That "something" of course had nothing to do with the bellboy.

However much we try, there are those inevitable moments when a strong emotion gets hold of us. We lose control of the situation. Only a great person can express a negative emotion for the right reason to the right degree at the right time. Unfortunately, most of us are not that perfect. Even if the reason seems right most of the time, the degree of reaction is excessive. What follows is an undesired consequence, regret and often some damage—even if we originally had just cause to be angry.

The bellboy had serious cause to be angry at the abusive behavior of the guest. But at that moment, the bellboy had the greater power between the two: the power to rein in his reaction.

Imagine a policeman being taunted by a crowd. The crowd waves fists, pushes him around, someone calls him names.

How does he decide, when he has the power of violent retribution in his hand and justifiable reasons to use it, what to do? Stare down the crowd, use a baton or use a bullet? How does he know how much is enough?

In extremely high-pressure situations, often the best emotion to express is control. And a true professional has a calibrated thermostat that prompts the degree of reaction and control required in any given situation.

# Chapter 17

# Welcoming Feedback

Most feedback, by its very nature, feels uncomfortable. This is because feedback is packaged as, or is perceived to be, personal criticism.

It is interesting to note that a sound technician treats all feedback as unwelcome noise. That is exactly how we feel when a customer or a senior colleague provides feedback. We gently thwart it in the sound studio of our minds. In the workplace we covet praise but gloss over most other feedback, even when we say we want to hear it for continuous improvement.

People are taught that every customer complaint presents scope for improvement. Yet scores of employees would rather not deal with an irate customer. How often do people read customer feedback in the raw and not in the aggregated form? How often do we read between the lines of a summary? How often do we travel to the customer's location and discuss negative feedback? Some never even know what their customers look like.

A very common instrument of feedback in many organizations is the 360-degree appraisal. In it, an employee is asked to choose a set of at least six peers and six subordinates, apart from the supervisor, to whom a questionnaire can be sent for feedback. We all have the urge to seek feedback from people who are more likely to say nice, reassuring things about us than make critical observations. That in itself is an insecure act and indicates a lack of maturity, of self-confidence to remain open to ideas and thoughts.

A professional craves real feedback. The ability to freely seek feedback, and more important to take feedback and act on it, is something that can only be learned over time. And it requires constant effort to master. But without developing this ability you cannot become a true professional.

As you practice the art of listening to feedback, you begin to pick it up when it is a whisper, like the sound of your own breathing, and you pick it up from unusual sources.

# Chapter 18

# Not Suffering False Attractions

You have just started working in your current organization. While applying for the job, you had indicated that you have made enough career changes and now want to settle down. At the interview, you went to great lengths to establish why this was the job and the kind of organization that you were really looking for.

You got the job. Three months into it a headhunter calls you. There is a new multinational in town and they are looking for someone with the same profile as yours. The job pays 50 percent more than what you currently make and according to the man at the other end of the line, it has great professional challenge.

That night you have trouble falling sleep. A lady named temptation visits you.

She whispers into your ear all the things wrong with your current assignment. She reminds you of noncooperation by your new colleagues. She eggs you on by reminding you that you have suggested pathbreaking ideas in the short time you have been there, but no one really listens to you in this new organization. She brings up the fact that you felt shafted when, after joining, you found out that some of your colleagues were earning more than you for doing the same job. Why then do you feel this false sense of virtue—as if you owe the organization something for hiring you?

It is not the false virtue, but the false attraction of which one must beware.

The fact of the matter is that you have not paid back your organization for taking a risk in hiring you just three months ago. The fact is that you did not anticipate the amount of effort you would need to make before being accepted by peers and subordinates. The fact is that, to the headhunter, you are just another head to hunt, to make his cut and bonus.

Flirting with false attractions makes us lose affection for what is on hand. If you do not have a serious need for the offered job or assignment, do the professional thing and resist the temptress.

# Chapter 19

# Never Lose Touch with Your Work

David Ogilvy, the founder of Ogilvy & Mather, one of the world's most respected advertising agencies, once beautifully described the idea of maintaining contact with your work when writing about his first mentor in the professional world. The man was the head chef at the Majestic Hotel in Paris. He had a retinue of assistants to cut, wash, cook and do all the things that were needed to make the restaurant's signature dishes. But this gentleman did something else to ensure that he earned respect as the boss. Occasionally, he cooked a dish, just to show his assistants that he still could.

As we advance in our organizations, we lose touch with the real work that goes on in them. As you start dictating notes, you lose your typing skills. As a senior surgeon, you stop operating and can no longer tie a suture as well as an intern can. As the head of a business division, you become so big that someone has to change your slides while you make presentations. You no longer do your own research; you cannot design your PowerPoint presentations. You stop making cold calls once you become VP of sales.

These are all signs of decay.

A professional does not let go of the basic ability to work because it is like losing your fingers. There are some things you must continue to do at any stage of your career. Not just the cerebral strategizing, but the actual work. For the chef, it's not about the presentation of the dish, but about how to handle the kitchen knife to make the perfect cut.

A few months before he retired, my father started what we thought was a weird practice. He picked up his own plate after every meal and washed it. He started washing his own clothes and cleaning the toilet. As a result, we had to follow suit. When asked why he was doing all this, he simply said, "Soon I will be a retired man." My mother, though blind for the greater part of her life, always washed her own clothes, made her own bed and swept the floor.

Doing what are often thought of as menial tasks has a calming effect on us. Doing the small things in life yourself is very important. These have greater significance than you know. Sometimes, the most profound ideas come not when you are in the boardroom but when you are washing dishes. So do not stop walking when you have a car. Do not stop driving yourself because you can be driven. Make your own slides. Write your own speeches. Go and make a cold call every now and then. Make an omelet or a cup of tea for yourself. And sometimes, get into the weeds at work.

## Chapter 20

# Being Proactive

Valmiki, the sage who wrote the Ramayana, counted the many essential qualities that make a great king. He saw them manifest in the personality of Lord Rama. One among them was the quality of being what he termed *agravashi*, or the one who initiates conversation. Imagine when two great individuals meet. Invariably, one of them makes a subtle, often brief, but observable, proactive stance—sometimes it is the first extension of the hand or the first spoken word. That seemingly trivial motion is the sign of a king. I believe that is also the sign of a true professional.

Being proactive is an amazingly wonderful attitude and a behavior that earns us memorable relationships in both life and business. Everyone loves to deal with a proactive individual. Every boss prays to have such a person on her team. What makes someone proactive?

First and foremost, like the king, a proactive person is self-confident. People who are unsure of themselves are unlikely to extend their hand first. This self-confidence is not about who you are; it is about where the conversation could lead. What if by extending my hand I end up committing to something? What if you ask me for something I cannot give or do not have? Fear of commitment makes us stay put, keeping the hand and the words to ourselves.

A proactive individual is genuinely interested in the well-being and welfare of the other person. One day, I got a call from my family doctor. A week before I had complained to him of back pain. He had prescribed a course of medication and now I was feeling fine. "Subroto," he started, "you have not been a good patient." He was admonishing me for my silence. In that moment, he was not really concerned about his fees or his medical practice. He genuinely wanted to know how I was faring and why I had not made the time to call.

Proactive individuals are not worried about creating work for themselves as an unwanted consequence of reaching out. Why fix something that isn't broken? Why nudge a customer who has not called for months about how the machine you repaired is working? What if it opens up a Pandora's box?

For all you know, the reason he has not called is that your competitor has offered to take back the bad equipment, scrap it and install his latest model—and has worked out a great financing deal your company has not even thought of!

Proactive behavior is about our small dealings in everyday life. It is about being the first. You could be the first to send a clipping of an article that could help a peer working on a related project when she is snowed under. You could be the first to reach out to the boss and request time to discuss your performance appraisal. You could be the first to analyze the price performance of a solution you installed for your customer a year ago. The first to write a point-of-view document for the firm, or the first to apologize when you butt heads with a colleague in a meeting.

In other words, you could be the first to be king! That is the power of proactive thought and action. Sometimes, being proactive can and will land you in trouble. But what kind of king is afraid of trouble?

Proactive people think on behalf of others. Sometimes it is also about thinking ahead of others. This attitude is then followed up by thoughtful preparation. If you analyze the reasons for attrition in the company before the bosses have woken up, guess who is the one spending nights researching the data? If you are about to suggest to your customer a new payment model that is good for her and good for you, who is the one spending time on the weekend doing spreadsheets?

There is another critical side to proactive behavior. In the world of business and professional dealings, people do not like to be taken by surprise. Anything that may cause grief if discovered must be brought to light by you, voluntarily, ahead of time and put in front of all the stakeholders who could be affected by it. It is uncomfortable while you do it but it builds lasting relationships.

Proactive behavior extends to our personal lives as well. Someone who is proactive at the workplace is more likely to be proactive with his health, and in his relationships with friends and family.

# Chapter 21

# Taking Charge

In 2003, as the chief operating officer of MindTree, I wanted to take my direct reports on an annual exercise to some place away from Bangalore, where the company is headquartered. The purpose of the exercise was to set out the objectives for the various departments I was responsible for. I wanted to tell them about my priorities for the future so that they could align their objectives with mine and with one another's. In the process, I also wanted them to share their functional goals with one another so that everyone was aware of what each department was doing.

The stated plan was to drive down in a small bus to a place in the middle of nowhere where my friend Captain Ravi, an ex–army officer, ran a highly successful outbound learning center called Pegasus Camp. There I wanted the team members to listen to one another, question, ideate and return with solid alignment and a collective vision for the year ahead.

Along the way, I also wanted to expose them to a situation involving extreme pressure and uncertainty so that they became emotionally ready for what I foresaw as an unpredictable time ahead. With Captain Ravi's help, I hatched a plan unknown to my colleagues.

The group assembled on the appointed morning for the bus ride. They were told that I would not be joining them as I had decided to go ahead by car. Only the bus driver knew what was to come.

An hour and a half into the journey, the bus turned off the highway onto a barely navigable road. The bus had to go past a tiny village before coming to the Pegasus Camp, which was located down a hill by a lake. When the bus approached the village, the managers, still somewhat sleepy and now weary from the rough-and-tumble journey, were accosted by angry villagers who had barricaded the road. The driver had no option but to stop, and as soon as he did, the mob surrounded the bus.

Apparently a car ahead of the group had mowed down a goat and sped off. The irate stick-and-sickle-wielding mob demanded that everyone get down from the bus and stay right there until the car owner returned to compensate the villagers for the loss of the goat. The group was stunned. The description of the car and driver suggested that I was the one who killed the goat. The villagers were relentless, their tempers rising by the second. They refused to engage in conversation and kept demanding that the group get down from the bus.

Away from the scene, inside the village school, I sat glued to a small window and watched the reactions of the people on the bus: fear and uncertainty. That bus had some very qualified, competent and senior managers onboard. People who reported to me were usually stars. They were trained to handle very difficult corporate situations; they were engineers and MBAs and trained negotiators.

But this situation was different. Here were villagers who did not speak English, were armed and angry and seemed like they could and would do anything if slightly provoked. I wanted to see how the leaders would react, who would take charge. The first reaction of the group was to stay put in the bus. No one stepped out.

After a while, a few of them tried reasoning with the mob from inside the bus. But it was futile because the group did not have a nominated leader and it is impossible to negotiate with a cacophonous bunch. Most of the managers just stayed in their seats, anxiety writ large on their faces. It was soon evident that the villagers were determined to get everyone out, and who knew what they would do next.

Then in the melee, I saw two men, Nagan and Sripad, slowly get up, come to the door of the bus, open it and get off. These two were not the most senior among the group; they were not the stars who would wow everyone with their presentations in the boardroom. They could best be described as somewhere between solid citizens and unsung soldiers. In that instance, however, where others were courting safety, these two men had waved aside all caution, putting group before self. As they cajoled the villagers, their captors got more menacing. Surrounded from all sides, they kept trying to pacify, to reason, standing between the villagers and the bus door, negotiating on behalf of their colleagues. At this stage, I came out of the village school with a goat in tow, and seeing me, the villagers stopped the premeditated drama. The mood in the bus changed from fear to jaw-dropping disbelief to relief and happiness. Later, we sat down to decode what had happened to appreciate the nature of unscripted events in the workplace.

Several years after the incident, many of the stars in the bus have either become dust or gone on to shine elsewhere; the two men who climbed out of the bus that day continue to serve Mind-Tree well. But to me, the goat that was never killed settled the issue as to who among the busload could be counted upon in case of a future crisis.

Faced with a potentially dangerous situation, people freeze. They are afraid to push their way into a crowd because they feel powerless. They justify their inaction by thinking that not being in the front, not taking charge of a dangerous situation is the wiser (and safer) thing to do.

We have often heard that no one can give you power, it has to be seized. While the first part of the statement may have a tinge of truth to it, the second is simply untrue. Power is not something material that you can seize, like a gun or a piece of land. Power is never seized. It is always generated from within. Whether you are powerful or powerless, you must feel these qualities before you can become them. Developing the power within, to have the confidence to take charge in the most difficult and potentially dangerous of situations, is the hallmark of a true professional.

# Chapter 22

# Courtesy and Humility

The chairman of Infosys, India's much talked about software services giant, N. R. Narayana Murthy entered the room with a young colleague and a guest. There were only two chairs in there. That morning, Murthy was somewhat preoccupied with his own thoughts. As Murthy and the guest settled down for a conversation, he took one chair, while the guest took the other. Only after the meeting was over did Murthy realize that his colleague had been standing the entire time, and Murthy felt terrible about the insensitivity he had shown.

In our discussions, Narayana Murthy has always stressed the importance of courtesy and generosity as a marker of professionalism. More important, you must show generosity and courtesy to people when you are in a position of power. Nearly two decades ago Murthy was nominated to receive an award instituted by a well-known charitable organization in western India. The evening before the award ceremony, he noticed a famous woman columnist and walked up to introduce himself. The lady simply looked through him. The next day, after he received the award, the lady told him that she had not known *he* was the recipient of the award when he had approached her the evening prior. Murthy simply replied, "Does it really matter?"

Many years later, a friend of Narayana Murthy's won a major award, and the same columnist happened to be at the party in his honor. This time she made it a point to walk up and talk to Murthy, who had by now become an internationally known figure, to inquire if he remembered meeting her a long time ago. Murthy politely said yes but also distinctly remembered how rude she had been when she was the better known of the two. Murthy sums up the issue by saying, "You're Amitabh Bachchan and you show grace and courtesy—that is when it matters. Not when you are just an aspiring actor." Generosity, grace and courtesy become truly valuable only when shown to others at the height of your professional career. (For those who do not know, Amitabh Bachchan is a living legend of Bollywood cinema and one of the greatest actors of all time.)

Professional adulation is like the beacon of a lighthouse—it falls on you for a few moments and then it must move on. People who think the spotlight will always remain on them, and are often rude, insensitive and self-absorbed, soon discover the loneliness of being in the shadows. Professionals must know that humility is critical to enduring success. When we are humble, we can listen to others. When we do, we remind ourselves of our weaknesses when others are discussing our strengths.

When you suspend humility, you only hear the adulation and it becomes regenerative until you turn deaf. Often it takes a personal tragedy to bring you back to normalcy, and that is an avoidable price to pay.

Murthy practices something very interesting to retain his

humility. Every night, before going to bed, he stays awake with the lights out for a few minutes to recall the mistakes he made during the day. During this time, he speaks to his conscience. Sometimes, when he has made a regrettable mistake, this process of recounting the incident is cathartic, because it makes him relive it and only then can he let go of the pain. Before he falls asleep, he prays that he should be given the strength not to repeat the same mistake.

There is a proverb in many Indian languages. There are three leaves—the one on top is falling, the one in the middle is trembling and the young one beneath is awaiting its time. In every profession, the ones on top should be aware that theirs is only a temporary accommodation.

Given the constant ebb and flow of our professional lives, it is important not only to have this humility but to have an appreciation for the potential in people below us—to recognize and nurture that special someone who right now is not quite there but may go further than you have. In Eastern culture, a certain respect for senior people comes rather naturally. A professional does not take this respect for granted.

Chapter 23

# The Big Picture

I was experiencing a mild but pestering pain in my left shoulder for a few days. Then one morning at work, I saw a colleague with a cast. What happened? I inquired. Lo and behold, he had a similar but more serious shoulder problem and had undergone surgery. Hearing him, I asked if I could see his doctor. I was visiting India for a few days from the United States at that time and requested an appointment right away.

The doctor overwhelmed me in the first meeting. He had read every single article I had ever written, as well as my books. After a brief examination during which he convincingly concluded that I had some kind of degeneration, the doctor informed me that a famous cricketer had the same problem, indicating that I was in exalted company and that surgery was in order. "How lucky I am to be able to operate upon you," he gushed.

Just to be sure surgery was needed, I had an MRI done the very next day. When I called my wife in the United States and informed her, being a very balanced person, she asked that I meet our family doctor in India before rushing into things, and I did that. Since

I was already under the spell of the scalpel, the family doctor sent the MRI reports to a sports doctor, who in turn confirmed that I had the same problem the famous cricketer had. Convinced of the diagnosis, the first surgeon I had met was now eager to put me under general anesthesia and get started.

My wife asked me to come back and get another opinion before doing anything.

Back in the United States, a land famous for commercially minded doctors, I made an appointment to see an orthopedic surgeon who ran a private practice near my home in New Jersey. He saw the scans I had done in India. Then he looked me straight in the eye and asked, "Mr. Bagchi, how old are you?"

"Fifty," I replied.

He went on to say that his job was to cut people open and get paid for it. And yes, the MRI did show some degeneration of the shoulder. But if at the age of fifty my body did not show signs of degeneration, when would it? He advised against any surgical procedure. I had to accept the signs of my body's aging.

"But will I be able to ride my bike, Doctor?" I feebly asked. "What if it pains?"

"No pain, no gain," he replied, and I was ushered out of his clinic.

It has been almost four years since this episode and the shoulder pain no longer bothers me as it once did. But through its discovery and resolution, I learned an amazing lesson about professionalism. As we look at data, we must also look at the big picture. Only the big picture, the context in which we live and work, makes the facts relevant. And it is only when we understand and actively look at the big picture that we will develop into grounded professionals.

# Part Three

# Professional Qualities

# Chapter 24

# Of Time, Body and Soul

I started working when I was barely nineteen. That was a good three decades ago. In the intervening years, I have grown up professionally, married, raised two children, started my own company, written three books, acquired hobbies like teaching, photography and biking, learned yoga and meditation, made friends, attended the occasional social event, and yet I have never felt that I have less time on hand. This may sound unusual to many people who groan, "I don't have the time to do the things I once liked," or "I cannot cope with my work and have problems with my work-life balance."

One cannot be a great professional unless one masters time. This is not a book on time management; there are countless books on that subject. While you should read some, I do not believe that you can learn to master time by simply reading about ideas. It is probably more effective to watch and learn from people who actually seem to manage their time well, and who feel productive and satisfied. I have met many such people, and if there is one primary quality they all share it is self-discipline. If you lack basic self-discipline, you will soon find that poor time management is just one of your many problems.

There are deeper issues that you must address before you can achieve success with time management.

Most important is the status of your health. Good health is critical to productivity. Poor personal health affects concentration and leads to a feeling of exhaustion. The people who complain most about lack of time ironically are people who are in the prime of their life, but probably in poor health. The key is to ensure that you pay attention to what you eat, how much you sleep, the exercise your body gets and the ways you unwind. Strange as it may seem, these basic things go a long way in expanding the time available to do things.

Pay attention to how much you eat. Most of us eat way more than is necessary. We have so many options now to eat out that we are not careful. I will never forget a conversation I had with the famous cardiac surgeon Dr. Devi Shetty, who told me that of all people, Indians have the highest risk of heart attack because they overeat. Genetically, the average Indian is designed to make do with much less food. But now there is abundance and, as a result of both availability and affordability, many Indians eat excessively, leading to coronary complications. For many people, consumption is what defines success and it begins with food.

Then there is the accepted notion that the best way to do business or bond with colleagues is to go out for a drink. Nothing is further from the truth. In my work, I often have formal dinners with visitors and clients. If a client likes to drink a glass of beer or wine over dinner, that is fine. I have never lost anything by abstaining. Never use your work as an excuse to drink.

Next to eating in moderation is the need to sleep well and

sleep adequately. Most young people who come to the workforce bring erratic sleeping patterns from their student days, and over time get into the cycle of sleep deprivation. Sleep is as important as diet and exercise to produce great work.

The forties are usually the peak years of a professional's work life. It is then that you are snowed under with work pressure, apart from increased expectations from your family. Very often, your day starts early and ends late. You probably travel ten days a month. You do not realize it, but all this consumes you from within. Begin to pace yourself, slow down. It is a great time to use techniques like yoga and meditation to sharpen the ability to do more by doing less. In other words, you need to know how to burn less energy to deliver the same level of productive work. Sometimes prayer, or a quiet period for reflection early in the morning or before you sleep, is just as helpful.

# Chapter 25

# Doing More by Doing Less

As young managers, people tend to be all over the place. Some simply revel in multiplicity. They have no time to pause and think. They thrive on multitasking, constantly checking e-mails, sending out text messages and calling their voice mail number while rushing to and from meetings or frantically trying to finish a project on time. In the process, many develop a state of mind in which volume of activity becomes more critical than the value one adds.

Doing more, being engaged 24/7, does not mean you are achieving more. As a professional, the trick is to do more by doing less. To do this, you have to disengage from doing too many things at the same time and prioritize based on where you can make a larger impact. The practice of disengagement from distractions becomes very important, particularly for midcareer professionals.

Strange as it may sound, a way to disengage from multiplicity is to learn something new—a sport, a foreign language or a musical instrument. Pick up something that regenerates you and revives the spirit of curiosity and learning in you. Give it undisturbed time.

As you move into your forties, it is time to become your own benchmark. It is time to bury past rivalries and disgruntlements about who got which promotion ahead of you. Make the time to actively mentor someone and groom a replacement—this enables expansion of roles, encourages thinking beyond the obvious and gives you more time to focus on larger issues. As you mentor someone you find yourself energized and are thus able to do more.

As we approach midcareer we find ourselves slowing down, not being able to keep up because we begin to develop a knowledge gap. Make an active effort to bridge this gap. In a knowledge-intensive world, the only way you can remain ahead is by learning. The sources of learning themselves may change as the compression of time takes place in your work life. You may have to pay attention to what you read, participate in industry bodies and interest groups and find newer ways to accelerate learning and absorption. Look for newer sources of learning as well as newer ways to learn. Meanwhile, cut down distractions. You know very well what they are in your own case.

# Chapter 26

# The To-do List

I cannot remember a time when I did not make to-do lists. Each morning, I look at what I need to accomplish that day, and in the evening I check off all of the things I did. It is my small victory over time. When we started MindTree, I decided to go a step further. I told myself that I would save the notebooks that contain my never-ending to-do lists and my diary for each year. As a result, I have accumulated the notebooks and the diaries—these have pride of place in my office. I do not think they are more precious than the work I have accomplished but they egg me on; they help me to know that I was in charge and that I did my best.

Many tasks on the list do not get done for days or sometimes weeks. Inevitably, when I have accomplished them I cross them out with a sense of victory. My to-do list is not just about work. While I cluster work-related things in a group, I also have a personal to-do list and it gets the same treatment. I write both lists on the same page of the notebook. It is unbelievable how powerful this simple tool can be.

The to-do list is nothing but a set of goals—not the big goals of life, but the small day-to-day ones that we have to get through on our way to achieving our vision. Goals have a powerful ability to shape our behavior, motivate us, create energy. Once you build goals, you enter the virtuous cycle by which when you are close to achieving a goal, newer goals appear, and this process keeps you going. This is the essence of the purpose-driven life. During a conversation with the Dalai Lama on where he got his power from, the great man told me, "Your purpose determines your power." The humble to-do list is the beginning of purpose and prioritization.

The issue some people face is not the absence of a goal, but rather the presence of too many and the lack of prioritization. I find many young people wanting to learn a new language, enroll in a personal development program, join a gym, read a book, write a blog, run a marathon and socialize, all at the same time. It is important to prioritize one's life. Ask what is really important to you. Also ask yourself why that thing is so important and whether you are willing to commit yourself completely to it.

# Chapter 27

# Saying No

It is surprising how the inability to say no results in time wasting, poor prioritization and the feeling of always being rushed and behind on deadlines. I am constantly surprised by the number of people who attend company meetings in which they have no interest. It is a criminal waste of human potential. Do not attend meetings just because you get invited to them; say no when you know you have no value to add to the discussions. You will be surprised how your forthrightness will eventually evoke admiration.

When you learn to say no to unimportant things, you have the time to take on a task in whose outcome you have a serious stake and in which you believe. Attend meetings in which you have a solid viewpoint and can add or receive value. And undertake travel that is necessary. Filling up an airline seat to fill time is not a good idea.

The inability to say no to their superiors is a major problem for many young professionals. Often it comes with unnecessary awe for a person in a position of power. A young doctor may feel compelled to drink with a senior surgeon who likes company. Young salespeople who look up to their older managers feel obliged to go along with the senior person's eccentricities. I would advise two things: never do anything you do not want to do, and learn to say no to additional chores or requests outside of work. If the senior is a professional, he will appreciate your candor. As a professional you must set the limits, and when you do, people will respect you for it.

# Chapter 28

# Quit Whining

Jobs are not meant to satisfy us. Jobs do not know who we are, what we are seeking and what our special needs could be. You may think this is a mere philosophical statement. On the contrary, I believe it is the most practical and rewarding way of looking at a professional's career. When I see scores of successful people around me, I believe that their achievements are due largely to such a perspective.

Some people dislike their work, some like the salary but not the work, some dislike their boss and yet others dislike their colleagues. In some cases people dislike the idea of work itself. A professional realizes that work is a blessing and, most of the time, it is therapeutic. We are lucky that we have work to do. Every day, increasing numbers of people in this world feel left out, unlucky, because they have woken up to a morning without any work. Go to villages anywhere in the world and you will realize what unemployment really means and how scores of people are grateful if they can manage even seasonal employment.

Many professionals argue that it is not the work they do that bothers them; they are bored with the routine. "I seek challenge" is the headline on most résumés. The world goes around because of its capacity to be predictable. The bees and other insects pollinate the crop so that we get our food with "monotonous" regularity. Imagine the sun getting bored with its work or the Earth feeling bored with its axis? Routine things done well make life livable.

And what is not routine about a cardiac surgeon who operates on people every day? Or a pilot who flies airplanes? At Bangalore's famous hospital, Narayana Hrudayalaya, doctors operate on newborn babies and infants who suffer from heart ailments. These small children must remain for days in the intensive care unit where every baby is assigned a dedicated nurse who keeps a watchful eye on the baby at all times. The hospital boasts a 95 percent operation success rate—not because of the doctors who operate and leave, but because of the nurses who take care of the babies after the operation. The job of the nurse is as routine and as predictable as it gets. But it is her work that ensures 95 percent of the children operated on would never have to return to a heart hospital. That is the definition of a 95 percent success rate at Narayana Hrudayalaya. The great challenging job is often an illusion; making the routine interesting is the real challenge.

Sometimes, we have very genuine problems at work. We may be underemployed or stymied in our quest for advancement, or have toxic bosses and difficult colleagues. The way out is to face up to the problem. Speak to someone in the organization or even an outside trained counselor. Discuss the issue, find a solution, be open in examining how much of the problem is because of you or your own insecurities. Try to correct yourself. If you find the organizational fit is wrong, find another job—but do not whine.

It simply does not help. When you whine about your workplace troubles, chances are two kinds of people listen—those who do not care anyway and those who are happy that you are in trouble.

If the solution is finding another job, be sure you are not going to an organization where you will encounter similar problems. Many people end up in the wrong profession because of lack of prior knowledge about it, and then they complain for the rest of their lives. It is never too late to start all over again. There are enough resources available to help you understand your aptitude. So it is never too late to find out what you are cut out for and re-align your job, rather than remain stuck and complain about your work.

There are situations, however, when high achievers tire out or simply outgrow their jobs. When the latter happens, there may be no visible external sign. No one is aware of the situation except you; only you know when you have outgrown your shoes because they pinch, and the same is true when you outgrow a job. When you see the signs of mental pinch, consider expanding your organizational role. Ask for additional responsibilities. Walk up to your boss and ask to take on more work. Consider spending time with younger colleagues. Build into your work elements of service—that will invariably make your job, and your achievements, more enriching.

# Chapter 29

# A Long View of Time

I first started writing for *Dataquest*, India's leading computer industry magazine, way back in 1982. It started with an occasional piece every now and then, but I took it seriously enough for the magazine to eventually offer me three consecutive columns to write. In the process I built personal visibility and a professional reputation that not only helped my work but also got me a job at Wipro Corporation. In the later years, as I grew in my professional life, I maintained my commitment to writing and eventually wrote a column called "Arbor Mentis" for *Businessworld* magazine. This column drew the attention of my publisher, and that is how I was given my first contract to write *The High-Performance Entrepreneur*. Around that time, Prashant Hebbar, former journalist at *Dataquest*, and Indrajit Gupta, my editor at *Businessworld*, joined *The Times of India*. Their goal was to revamp the business page of the number-one newspaper in the country. As part of it they wanted a human-centric column that would make the nonbusiness reader "stray into and stay" on the business page. Hebbar had followed me for a decade and

Gupta had interacted with me closely while at *Businessworld*. They asked me to write a new column, "Times of Mind." It soon became one of the most talked-about columns in the Indian media. When Indrajit Gupta left *The Times of India* to become the first editor of *Forbes India*, he asked me to write "Zen Garden," my biweekly column in the magazine. Similarly, after writing *The High-Performance Entrepreneur*, I was commissioned to write *Go Kiss the World*, and the success of both books has now led to *The Professional*.

The reason I am sharing this with you is twofold: I believe that one must take a long view of time in building any professional relationship. It goes well beyond the work you produce at your job. My relationships with Hebbar, Gupta and my editor at Penguin are not just about writing but about how, over time, we have engaged with each other, how we have ideated, ironed out differences and co-created valuable work. If working with each other was not a pleasure, something we were jointly committed to for the long term, we would not have continued our relationships, and would have moved on to other choices. It is the power of association that builds formidable value over time, which the myriad other choices cannot provide.

The second point I want to make is the importance of taking every assignment seriously. Whether I wrote a regular column, an occasional newspaper piece or for that matter a book, I gave it all I had. To me, my writing commitments were no different from commitments at work. This attitude called for many personal sacrifices because it was always like having two jobs. Yet the rewards have been huge.

Every professional's footprint must be larger than his daytime job. Our professional identity goes well beyond the employment badge we wear at work. So while dealing with people who may be suppliers, customers, industry associates and other stakeholders, one must build a long view of time and treat every small engagement with them with all seriousness, as if life depends on it.

Chapter 30

# Mavens, Connectors and Evangelists

Among the most powerful things you can have as a professional is a strong network. A good network, cultivated wisely and used well, is a great expander of time. It can achieve great things for you. To make it work for you, you need to know two things: First, you have to contribute value to a network before you can get value from it. Second, its primary job is not to give you the ability to meet your targets in the short term. In other words, a network needs to be cultivated with a long view of time. One needs to understand how to use it wisely and well.

A good network can bring you in minutes what hours of individual research may not. In many organizations today, leaders encourage people to form voluntary communities. There are stories galore in knowledge-based companies of how someone in the United States reaches out to the global community of fellow professionals late at night with a request for help and solutions arrive in his mailbox the very next morning from people far away in Australia or India. When you acquire the reputation of being a contributor of value to a community, you are invariably flooded with high-quality help when you need it.

I have my own short list of favorite professionals—doctors, journalists, economists, filmmakers, architects, young entrepreneurs—whom I reach out to routinely, seeking their advice on dozens of matters. You may think for a moment, What is so great about this? Isn't this the same thing as using your world of contacts to help you get things done?

To me these people are not "contacts," they are "connectors." The world of a professional consists of what we call mavens, connectors and evangelists. A maven is someone who produces, consumes and trades knowledge. A group of mavens is usually connected to an expert who is called a connector. A connector provides clarification, assistance and linkages to other connectors. A group of connectors may link up to an evangelist, who is the last word in a particular field of knowledge. In a world of mobile devices, the Internet and information overload, these people can substantially cut down research and consulting time, which is precious to me. Without them I would have to do hours and days of work, whereas these people can guide me effortlessly to the precise point of knowledge or expertise, or provide me with a counteropinion. You do not build a network of such professionals through the low-level principle of trading favors. In fact, such people would dislike the very idea. Interaction with them is governed by the principle of mutual respect and affection which is built over years.

# Chapter 31

# White Space

Every day, as I hit Bangalore's busy Inner Ring Road, I look for my favorite sight: a three-wheeler converted into a delivery van with the words EGG VAN written on it. Presumably, the owner is in the egg business and uses this vehicle to deliver eggs to retailers in the city. But when I see the Egg Van, it is not loaded with eggs. It has a shutter at the back which is open a foot above the fender. Through it, the sun filters in and I see two young girls, dressed in school uniforms, sitting cross-legged with books open on their laps. Between them, I see their schoolbags. I have never seen their faces but I can imagine their eyes. The picture uplifts me in an instant. On the same road, I see countless office buses that ferry bored young men and women with tired looks on their faces, some sleeping, others switched off from the world via a pair of white earplugs.

I call the two girls my "angels of white space." I do not know how the term "white space" originated, but in telecommunication, it denotes frequency allocated to a channel but not used. Typically, broadcasters are provided additional frequency that is not meant to be populated so that adjacent broadcast stations do not overlap. In print, a white space denotes emptiness so that we can read the characters that form a word and a group of words that form a sentence.

In our professional lives, white space is a train or a bus ride to work, it is the time waiting outside a client's office, the time spent on long flights. We have all been given huge white spaces and we simply let their power go to waste. I am not suggesting that we cram work into every available moment. Quite the contrary, these white spaces should be an oasis of recreation and rest. Mindless use of time that neither helps get work done nor rests the mind is a waste; use your white space for getting things done in a planned, proactive manner. Find your own angels of white space.

Chapter 32

# Creating Reuse

Whenever you create something useful, always consider how you can reuse it.

You're preparing an internal presentation to your sales team on sales productivity. A little bit of tweaking and generalization would probably make it a great training resource for the sales school your company runs or a valuable download to offer on your Web site. Offer the piece to a trade journal. Convert the idea into a white paper.

An internal memo to the organization on how to protect customers' intellectual property could become part of a point-of-view paper that could be used as a handout. While Mind-Tree's integrity policy is an internal document, it is also a great thing to showcase each time someone asks us about corporate governance.

By looking at what you are creating—an essay, a PowerPoint presentation, a policy document—as something that can be re-used, you can expand time and get more done in your day.

Reuse is about building components at work wherever possible so that we do not do the same thing over and over again. It is also about recognizing that everyday artifacts have multiple purposes.

The downside, however, is twofold: First, wanton reuse builds a "cut-and-paste" culture in which advice and resources are created with one party in mind but sometimes get reused on another party that might not benefit in the same way. Second, unless one is careful, there can be issues with intellectual property.

Reuse of work artifacts is a great way to expand time. Vast amounts of knowledge just sit in the content management system of an organization, yet professionals spend enormous amounts of time reinventing the wheel.

# Chapter 33

# What Is Your Touch Time?

In a factory, amid the countless activities that keep a manufacturing person busy, all that truly matters is when the raw material physically touches the machinery. It is only at that point, as the material converts itself into the next higher stage in production, that value is added. While a factory head may feel proud of the state-of-the-art machinery in his factory, what truly matters is not its capacity but the touch time the factory is able to achieve. Similarly, every professional must know the equivalent of touch time in his field. We are all busy doing things that fill up our workday, but these do not necessarily add up to touch time.

Once, I ran a study involving more than three dozen salespeople over a number of months during which they agreed to maintain logs of their activities for each day. I decided to conduct the study because they were all complaining about how stressed they were, how they did not have enough time to make new sales calls, or submit expenses, and certainly no time to feed customer information into the order processing system or chase accounts receivable. What was their principal gripe? That they had to perennially follow up with the manufacturing unit for product shipment. They complained that they were always on the phone speaking to the factory about delivery and short shipments. So we agreed that everyone would log their activities to see how much time they spent "following up with the factory" every day and how big this issue really was.

After the data was processed, the results surprised everyone. To begin with, the follow-up with the factory was taking less than 20 percent of their total time. Even though this was high and could be significantly reduced with systemic changes, it was nowhere near the amount of time the salespeople had imagined it to be. The study turned up other interesting data as well. The actual face time the salespeople had with potential customers was less than 12 percent of their total time—they all thought it was three times as much! For salespeople, face time with a prospect is the real touch time. Salespeople often forget to focus on this touch time, believing that time spent traveling, waiting in office reception rooms or making small talk with the receptionist is core sales activity.

Time expands only when we measure our value-added activities. The amount of time every white-collar worker wastes on unproductive activities adds up to quite a bit at the end of a day, week and month. Anyone who sings the refrain that he works really hard must step back and measure his touch time.

I work with high-achievement individuals to help them build their leadership capacity by working on self-awareness. An essential aspect of the process is an analysis of how they are spending their time. I urge them to look at a hard copy of their previous ninety-day calendar at any time. Most people who complain about not having enough time have many "not-so-hidden" time wasters.

People come to the office only to immediately go for a coffee break; smokers spend on average an hour a day taking nicotine breaks. People also attend unnecessary meetings. They surf the Internet and answer personal e-mails while at work. While some may argue that none of these things may be in the way of someone's productivity and may actually help some, we must be aware of the amount of time in a day we spend doing these things, and how they could be taking away from the time we need to do more valuable tasks.

When I ask people what they do when they are not working, many draw a blank and some say they watch television. Ask them what they watch and how much time they spend in front of the television, and you get a very evasive "This and that, not much time" in reply. Ask them to quantify the time in front of the television and it can be six to eight hours a week. Watching television can be relaxing and informative, but so can reading a book, or meditating—doing things to gain a complete body-mind-soul makeover.

Senior professionals who are productive and get things done on a sustained basis do four things particularly well. They get briefed, they seek help, they use commute time effectively and they periodically take a mental shutdown.

Given the information abundance we all experience, there is a pathological need to consume information by reading reports. As one goes higher up the ladder, the effective use of aides not just to take instructions but to absorb information and synthesize on your behalf, and sometimes even offer a viewpoint, can be very useful.

Seeking help is a great way to expand time. It is amazing how much idle time is available in any organization. In MindTree, there are people who are always waiting for a project to come through, and every time I need research done, I invariably reach out to such people. The call for help energizes them as much as it expands my time. Organizations that promote the culture of a "capacity market" in which people can notify one another who is available at any point in time actually increase productivity and at the same time build thriving communities that bond.

Apart from all this, it is very important to take periodic shutdowns. Many people complain about lack of personal time but the idea of a shutdown gives them withdrawal symptoms. Professionals who take compulsory breaks at regular intervals are able to get more work done, in less time, because of the power of a relaxed mind and body.

Chapter 34

# When Paths Diverge

In today's world, it is unrealistic to think that you will remain a one-job or two-job professional through a forty-year career span. I have made my fair share of job changes but I find that the places where I have made a recognizable impact are the ones where I spent five to ten years or more. Such a thing obviously requires a high degree of alignment between the individual and the organization. When we talk of that, usually people emphasize the organizational priority to get the right people in. But I believe that it is as much the individual's responsibility as it is the institution's. Good people tend to go to good organizations.

If you are any good, you should know that you have the right to outgrow your job after you have made an impact, you have the right to occasionally get bored and you have the right to covet more space. There's nothing wrong with seeking and making a job change. But a true professional makes sure he has thought through the consequences, sees the big picture, knows how to make the change and finally does not burn bridges while parting ways.

There is a great deal of similarity between a job and a marriage. You never simply marry someone, you marry into that person's family. The same is true of a job. It is not merely the job, but the organization that you are going to join. A great job in an organization that does not align with your values is a waste of your time. Another way to look at this connection is to think of the job as the house you want to move into and the organization as the neighborhood. A great house in a bad neighborhood may not be that great of a house after all.

If the neighborhood is great, you can progressively move to a better house someday. If you have really outgrown your job but are value-aligned with your organization, you may just need to find another place in the same company in order to make an even larger impact.

Sometimes it still doesn't work, and one must change jobs.

It's important to understand that most job changes do not change you. If there is an inherent incapacity that is not getting you the raise and the promotion in your current job, you will not solve the problem by simply switching organizations. Fix the gap, and if you cannot, come to terms with it. Do not fool yourself with the idea that a mere job change, just because it is possible, is going to solve your woes.

Always do a reference check. Reference checks are not the employer's prerogative alone. Ask the recruiter for the names of people who might be willing to talk to you and help you understand the new organization. Reach out to customers, suppliers and ex-employees. Look for patterns that prove or disprove what you read on the Web site. Say that you would like to spend a day at the proposed workplace before signing the acceptance letter.

While you do your due diligence, also know the trade-offs. If you so badly want double the compensation overnight, do not complain about office politics at the new place.

Once you have landed your new job, make sure you set it up for success. Try to blend in and not blend out in the initial days. Build value before seeking recognition. And do not make comparisons. As in any new relationship, so in a job, it is downright irritating for the new "spouse" to hear how heavenly your ex was.

Do not prey on your last employer. Everyone has a hard time not hiring an ex-colleague who has been their absolute favorite, or staying away from an ex-customer. To build your future at the cost of the previous organization, destabilizing it, leaving it hollow as you move on, is not professional conduct.

And most important, professionals always take the goodwill of everyone with them when they leave. You never know when you may need to come back as an employee, a customer, a supplier or simply a mutual reference.

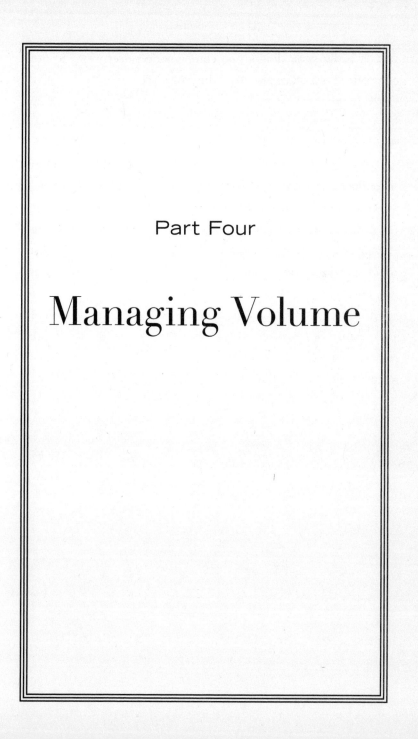

Part Four

# Managing Volume

# Chapter 35

# The Power of Vision

K. Srinivasan was a village postmaster in the erstwhile Madras State in 1957. A contented man in all respects, he had just one personal regret—he had never attended college. When his first child was born, he had the dream that his son would one day become an engineer. In the years ahead, there were two real constraints: the villages he got posted to often did not have a good school. He decided his wife and children must stay in one place where there was a good school for the sake of the children's education, and they would not accompany him on his transfers. This brought up the second constraint—having to pay for two homes. In order to avoid the additional expense he decided that, instead of renting a house for himself whenever he was traveling, he would simply sleep in the village post office, which was usually nothing more than a mud hut. The post office benefited as much as Srinivasan did. Even in his sleep he could hear the telegraph machine, and if the Morse code chatter revealed bereavement in some family, he would immediately get up and go convey the message, even in the middle of the night.

Srinivasan's son Janakiraman did well in the vernacular school he was studying in, and won a scholarship to the Regional Engineering College at Trichy, which is now among India's best engineering schools. From there, he went on to do his master's at the Indian Institute of Technology, Madras, before starting life as an R&D engineer. Eventually he became the chief executive of R&D at Wipro. That is how I met Janakiraman (affectionately known as Jani), who was to become a cofounder of MindTree.

Jani's story is about a father's dream, a vision. That vision made him sacrifice his own personal comforts and the joy of seeing his child grow up in front of his eyes, but he did it in order to realize his biggest dream—that of seeing his son get a great college education and grow into a successful adult.

A personal vision is an inherently powerful thing. The word "vision" has its origin in the Latin word *videre*, which means "to see." But at a deeper level it refers to an unusual competence in discernment or perception, intelligent foresight; it is the manner in which one sees or conceives of something. It is also said to be a mental image produced by imagination and a mystical experience of seeing as if with the eyes of the supernatural.

Vision is not about the past. Vision is not about the present. Vision is, almost invariably, a distant image of the nonexistent thing we call the future. It is the result of a mental process that telescopes a person into an image that simply does not exist in current reality. From then on, that image becomes the guiding factor. It helps build energetic action. As if tied to it by an invisible string, the person is slowly pulled forward by it, until the imaginary picture and life's reality become one.

Most visions bring with them what is called the "burden of

dreams." This idea is most appropriately depicted in the 1982 Werner Herzog movie *Fitzcarraldo*. The movie is about a man possessed by the idea of bringing the opera to the rain forest, which is considered sheer madness by everyone around him. He had no personal means, but undertook a hazardous journey up the Amazon to claim rubber estates so he could fund the building of a European-style opera house in Iquitos, Peru. His dream was a burden that brought him despair, banishment, rejection and unimaginable obstacles, including brushes with death. Yet he persisted until his dream was fulfilled. If you get a chance, see the movie.

Dr. Govindappa Venkataswamy was a gynecologist. He suffered from rheumatoid arthritis and watched helplessly as his fingers slowly became twisted and permanently warped, making him unfit to deliver babies. Instead of ruminating on this cruel twist of fate, he reeducated himself, this time in ophthalmology. He trained his twisted fingers to handle surgical tools and became so deft as an eye surgeon that he could perform a hundred operations a day! Then, at fifty-seven, his retirement orders came. But instead of getting shelved in a corner and slowly fading away, he opened an eleven-bed eye hospital in a rented house in Madurai, India, because he wanted to do something to help the rural poor who were becoming blind due to completely avoidable reasons.

From this humble beginning grew the legend of Aravind Hospitals. Today, collectively, the five Aravind hospitals see 2.4 million patients a year and perform an astounding 300,000 operations a year, of which 70 percent are done free of charge. Dr. V, as he came to be called, said in an interview with *Fast Company* magazine, "If Coca-Cola can sell billions of sodas and McDonald's can sell billions of burgers why can't Aravind sell millions of sight-restoring operations and, eventually, the belief in human perfection? With sight, people can be freed from hunger, fear and poverty. You can perfect the body, then perfect the mind and the soul, and raise people's level of thinking and acting."

Dr. V died in 2006. The power of his vision is embodied in the fact that its beneficiaries are twice, three times, even four times removed from him. None of the 300,000 people annually who have their sight restored are related to the man. That is exactly what guarantees the continuity of Aravind's success.

To me, Dr. V symbolized the ultimate professional.


I call people like my cofounder, Jani, children of vision.

Most of us begin life with the vision of a parent, a relative, often a teacher—these visions inspire us to study a particular subject, choose a profession or take up something that becomes our calling. We all grow up as children of that vision. Yet countless among us lose our power to dream and act as we subsequently settle down into a well-paying career.

Our professions are instruments to build and deliver value to others. What good is an instrument in the hands of a person who has no vision?

Vision is what vision does. American futurologist Joel Barker tells us that it is not enough to have a dream. You have to act on that vision. Vision without action is far less noteworthy than action without vision. Every day countless people imagine possibilities for our future—from a world free of hunger and poverty to acing a test to owning an island—but very few act, thereby reducing a potential vision to a mere daydream.

Vision must be acted upon; it must be externalized and articulated. And if it involves other people, it must encompass and include them, building what Barker calls a vision community. In the end, the worth of the vision is in its executed reality.

Many professionals, themselves children of great vision, lose the way somewhere and give up on their visioning capacity, which then becomes a recessive gene. Some lose it out of lethargy, some allow material success to submerge it. Yet there are others who abandon it as they face obstacles and blame their environment for it. All of us must understand one vital truth: it is the job of the environment to present obstacles. That is the way nature is built.

Nature designs things in such a way that dreams must die in the same proportion that wild salmon breed. Out of the 2,500 eggs a wild coho salmon lays, 2,125 die. Which is to say only 375 eggs hatch. Of these, only 30 survive. From this lot, 25 are either eaten by predators or die due to environmental reasons. Eventually, only 2 survive to become fully grown adults, to return to their source with the burden of their dreams and spawn. The same ratio applies to anyone who builds a vision that is larger than life. Just because you are a hatched salmon does not mean you are guaranteed safe passage to the ocean and back.

Professionals who have a profound vision are able to uplift not only their own lives but also the lives of those around them. As a professional, bring the power of vision to your work, and act upon it. Do not be fazed by the size of your adversary; the size of your adversary determines the size of your success.

# Chapter 36

# Affective Regard

*The American Heritage Science Dictionary* defines values as "beliefs of a person or social group in which they have an emotional investment." The same source defines values in sociology as "the ideals, customs, institutions, etc. of a society toward which the people of the group have an affective regard. These values may be positive, as cleanliness, freedom, or education, or negative, as cruelty, crime, or blasphemy."

I think both definitions merit attention. The first one tells us that values are personal. They are an emotional investment.

The second definition talks about affective regard. Values are not imposed to enslave us, and must be embedded in groups to which we belong. The profession we are trained in and the organization we work for are the two foremost groups in which we need to invest our values and build affective regard. A profession is not to be treated as an ATM or a gambling den. We need to build a value-centric view of our profession. A value-centric view can be built only by people who are capable of emotions.

According to Peter Drucker, the father of modern management, values provide us with constancy of purpose. There can be no profession without a set of professional values. When those values are transgressed, the professional mantle is disfigured, maimed and left in a state of sacrilege, as we saw in the examples of the doctor who sold kidneys and the lawyers who attempted to buy a witness in the earlier part of this book.

When we subscribe to a profession, it is to the exclusion of other options and it signifies a social membership. As a result, people who belong to a professional group must agree to abide by a set of values that makes the group both cohesive and worthy of societal respect. That is why every profession articulates its own set of professional values that are basic and form its core—these values do not vary across organizations related to that profession. If these values are violated, it amounts to desecration of the covenants of that profession. Thus for a medical professional, nonrefusal to treat a person in need is an inviolable covenant. For a lawyer, client confidentiality is nonnegotiable. For an army officer, the safety and honor of soldiers at war is a core covenant of that profession.

Values sometimes get internalized only when value transgressions take place. Through a negative set of examples people learn what is and what may not be acceptable behavior. These examples help members of a profession understand what it means to belong because human beings often have problems with abstractions and it is in the storytelling that we seek answers to our questions.

At MindTree, no one is called an employee. We do not like the term. We call ourselves MindTree Minds. When the company started, we asked each MindTree Mind what kind of an organization they wanted to build. From the many attributes that came up, we coalesced a set of five values that define a MindTree professional: Caring, Learning, Achieving, Sharing and Social Responsibility (CLASS). Caring meant caring for customers, people, financial stakeholders and the organization. In that order. Learning meant personal development and emphasis on building a spirit of innovation. Achieving was about aspiration, accountability and action orientation. Sharing meant teamwork, building knowledge and encouragement and, finally, social responsibility stood for being socially minded, imbibing the spirit of integrity and displaying commitment.

Even today, more than ten years later, every MindTree Mind attends a value session on joining. These sessions are usually run by Ashok Soota, the chairman. When the chairman of an enterprise explains why values are central to the people who have just joined the organization, most people get the message.

Not stopping there, we integrate the values at three additional levels—at the level of recruitment, at the level of performance appraisal and at the level of the annual 360-degree feedback. Despite all that, we realize that good intentions are not enough. In any growing organization, value transgressions are bound to happen. In such moments, how the organization behaves determines subsequent value enculturation.

In India, tax laws permit deduction at source for leave travel assistance twice every four years. By law a claimant must furnish actual proof of travel to claim the money. It is a widespread practice in government offices and in the private sector alike for people to furnish false documents that are easy to procure and claim the money without undertaking any travel. In most organizations, it is not looked down upon because the individual is only defrauding the tax authorities and not the organization itself. But regardless of who is defrauded, the fact is, submitting a false claim is a forgery. At MindTree, whether the taxman comes or not, you claim a tax exemption only if you have indeed incurred an expense. No ifs, ands or buts here. People who are not comfortable with such a position do not join MindTree.

One year, MindTree hired a thousand people, and to our utter dismay we found that as many as eighty of them had faked employment information in their résumés. One had submitted inflated salary information which, when verified at the source, turned out to be untrue. Another claimed to have worked in a company that did not exist or was just an employment certificate issuing scam. We asked them all to leave, even though from a technical standpoint these people had cleared our tests. Their social belief that you can bend the rules, fake information to get ahead in life and do what others are doing even if you know it's wrong did not fit in with our core values.

In yet another case, a MindTree Mind working at a client location was shown a competitor's proposal. That evening, he returned to the client's office, and using his access rights copied the proposal and submitted a competitive bid that we ended up winning. The story came out after his subordinates exposed it and questioned the ethics of the act. By then, work with the client had commenced. We removed the MindTree Mind from service and went to the client and informed him about the breach immediately. The client was shocked and saddened. After all, the individual was very valuable to the client, as he was to us. Removing him meant serious dislocation, and such abrupt changes in a project's composition invariably have other implications. But the person had taken a risk that compromised the basic values of the organization, and the issue had to be dealt with without worrying about the inevitable business consequences.

Value transgressions happen for a variety of reasons, and as long as an organization is in business, people will test its boundaries. Most times, the people who breach professional values are the most unlikely candidates, evoking responses ranging from "Are you sure it was him?" to "I never knew she could do such a thing" or "Why did he have to do it?"

At MindTree we have a simple precept. A value transgression is a value transgression—there is no shade of gray here. Irrespective of who is involved and what the impact will be on our bottom line, we part ways. We have been asked about the role of forgiveness in such situations. We believe forgiveness does not really work when it comes to a matter of values. Assume someone has faked a voucher or has sexually harassed someone. Even as you forgive the transgression, people will end up hearing about it and most likely will lose respect for that person. At MindTree we believe it is better for someone who has breached integrity to move out of the organization. That way the individual can make a fresh and hopefully clean start someplace else. Letting such people continue in the organization does not help because both their reputation and their self-respect have already been dented. Years after MindTree was started, we realized that value enculturation remained a challenge, partly because of the social system. We came up with the idea of the Integrity Book, also known within the company as the White Book. This book outlines the integrity policy of the organization, but goes a step further. Unlike organizations that keep their skeletons in the cupboard, we periodically publish them—we reveal the instances of value breach and how the matter was dealt with. This book can be downloaded from the MindTree Web site and is freely distributed among colleges we recruit from and other organizations, including our competitors.

It is the duty of top management to propagate the organization's values through personal behavior and demonstrate the price the organization is willing to pay from time to time to defend what makes up its core. In countries like India, it is extremely critical that there is an organizational framework available so that people can easily relate to the idea. But there are countless self-employed professionals who do not have the advantage of such a framework and are invariably left to their own means. For them, it is a tougher battle when choosing what is right over what is convenient because they lack an effective system that can clarify value questions.

The self-employed professionals in every society have the maximum opportunity to run their vocation without their income being tracked, unlike a salaried individual. The easiest temptation is tax evasion. From that point onward, some people feel bold enough to do worse things. Left to self-regulation, people fail easily because they are also witness to too many of society's wrongdoings and it is very difficult to remain on the straight and narrow. Once they cross the boundary, it becomes a downward spiral for many.

A doctor becomes part of an insurance fraud. A real estate agent withholds critical information from a client. A lawyer bribes a judge. In each instance, the professional breach is justified as the price to be paid to be part of a system. The truth is, every time it is an individual choice.

•   •   •

Seldom does sticking to your values lead to great glory or high praise. Sometimes a personal price has to be paid in the practice of professional values, but in the end, those who stand by their convictions have a better opinion of themselves, which is far more important than any outside view. Society on the whole may not always put a premium on professional values, and hence most people do not incorporate them into their lives. But practicing professional values is about who you are and what you want to be known as—a professional or merely professionally qualified. And, in the end, even the most corrupt society hails the individuals who choose to be different.

Chapter 37

# Commitment to Commitment

As I finished my keynote address at an event in New Delhi, the usual enthusiastic group of young entrepreneurs, press persons and students rushed forward with business cards in hand, their eager faces wanting to snatch a few strands of conversation or the promise of a private meeting later.

A young journalist from a national magazine insisted that we speak for a few minutes. She needed to file a story but I had a flight to catch right after the talk. I asked her to send me her questions by e-mail instead, promising her a rapid turnaround. She accepted, and we agreed that I would respond the same day. On the ride to the airport and while waiting to board a flight, I invariably spend time reading and answering e-mails, so that day, I anticipated receiving her questions and was mentally prepared to respond as quickly as I could.

At the same venue, as I was leaving, a young woman introduced herself as a social entrepreneur. She said that she had come all the way from Chennai to listen to me speak and she wanted to discuss a few things face to face. As I was on my way to her city, I asked her to call me the very next morning when we both would be in Chennai, to arrange a time to meet. She noted my number and gave me hers.

The next morning, I woke up remembering my promise to her but realized I had not yet received a call from her. After I got ready for the day, I decided to call her instead. A sleepy voice answered the phone. It took her a while to realize who was on the line. Then she told me she had stayed back in Delhi to visit her mother. She had obviously not taken my offer to meet the very next day in Chennai seriously.

From Chennai, on my way back home to Bangalore, I was burdened by my promise to reply to the eager journalist's questions. I checked my mail; there was nothing from her. After I reached home, I downloaded mail again. Nothing. Again after dinner I checked my computer and found nothing from her. I even checked my junk mail folder on the off chance her mail had been quarantined as spam. Nothing. She had not sent her questions.

The next morning I decided to call her. When she answered, she was completely taken aback that it was me on the line. It was clear that after our short conversation she had erased the idea of sending me the questions from her mind. I could feel her embarrassment. I had taken her by surprise.

What these two young "professionals" lacked was commitment, or rather commitment to commitment. It is unlikely that I will ever take them seriously if our paths cross in the future.

We tend to think of commitment as a larger-than-life thing, to be reserved for grand gestures like going off to fight a war for the sake of the country. For every soldier, though, his commitment to his country is in the details of his everyday work—in his punctuality, his appearance, his responsiveness and task completion every step of the way. A soldier does not go to war every day, but his commitment to perform every small task decides victory when the big day arrives.

This quality to do what you have said you will do, in the time you have committed to do it, must be applied to the smallest of tasks in your life. Without it, you not only disrespect others, you disrespect yourself.

Without commitment we cannot achieve even small successes, much less large ones. Without commitment, we cannot give our best to our organization. And without commitment, we cannot turn our vision into reality.

Chapter 38

# Be Prepared

---

Great professionals are always prepared—for conversations, meetings, presentations. Prepared individuals project a good image of their company and of themselves, which is the first step toward making a client feel important. Imagine going to a doctor, a lawyer or an accountant and having to repeat everything you had discussed in your previous meetings. On the other hand, when your doctor begins by saying, "The last time we spoke about a change in diet, your exercise regimen and a shift from a high dosage of your medicine down to a maintenance level . . ." you already know that you are in good hands, and have the confidence that your doctor is the best.

In contrast, think about all the times you've had to explain your problem to a customer service representative when you called the toll-free help line number of any service provider. You would feel far less frustrated, better served and more satisfied in the end if you didn't have to repeat your problem each time.

A professional architect will bring along sketches and concepts from the last meeting, and a summary of the points discussed.

. We have rich evidence of how these ideas were used
 to seek information, knowledge and even the ultimate
he concept of asking a question to get to the bottom of
as often propagated through storytelling. Unfortunately,
tion seems to have lost its way in the modern education
we have designed for ourselves. Our education system,
t of the society we live in, discourages questioning and
 in an effort to mass-produce thousands of engineers,
awyers, management graduates and others with so-called
nal qualifications. Doctors and lawyers are required to
tioning as part of their daily work, yet the art and science
oning is really found only in a few among them.

bility to ask questions, no matter what field you work in,
al for success. When I went to learn Total Quality Man-
(TQM) in Japan in the 1990s, I came across the concept
ven Quality Control (QC) Tools, which included Japanese
nent guru Kaoru Ishikawa's fishbone diagram. This is a
oot cause analysis (RCA) among management profession-
 so called because when fully drawn, the diagram looks
keleton of a fish.

dea is profoundly simple yet powerful. It suggests that
 tend to look at everything in a cause-effect manner and
onclusions based on what may be an apparent cause, and
oot cause, behind an event or a phenomenon. When you
n apparent cause of a problem, your efforts do not yield
e results. So the trick is to go deep enough until you find
ause and then consider a solution that truly removes the
t the core.

this, managers need to keep digging for facts or data
oot cause is unearthed and then apply their minds to the

A professional salesperson will go over his meeting notes from a previous call before visiting a client, which is why it is also important to take notes in a meeting and have them handy for the next one. And this is not just for the external world. It is equally important to circulate minutes of an internal meeting, if you are responsible for the meeting.

I would never meet someone without having researched him, especially considering how easy it is these days. Go to Wikipedia or LinkedIn, Google him, read the last annual report of the company, visit the company's Web site. If you do not have the time, subcontract the research to a young intern or a junior colleague who has a spare cycle. In the process, you not only become prepared, you spread the culture.

I always tell salespeople that you must "arrive before you arrive." And sometimes, in some miraculous way, when you work really hard and spend time thinking in preparation for a meeting, the message reaches the other party even before you actually arrive for the meeting.

Like the time MindTree had been trying to break into the preferred list of suppliers of a Fortune 500 company. We were doing some work for that company at the fringes but were not one of the five partners the company engaged with for big deals. And I was to call on the head of corporate procurement to exhort him to make us a partner of preferred choice. For days I simulated the meeting. I asked myself why on earth should he meet me? Why should he be sympathetic? What would make our meeting memorable when he is inundated by endless sales pitches?

The night before the meeting, the Oscar awards were announced. *Slumdog Millionaire* walked away with eight Oscars. I got my entry line for the next day's meeting. I decided to tell the executive two things: Who ever thought that one day the United States could have an African American as president, and who ever thought "Jai Ho"—the signature song of the movie—would be on the lips of everyone in the world? My subsequent pitch was based on the idea of change and why it was a good idea for him to let the underdog in.

You will be amazed at what happened the next morning. After I entered the executive's room and we exchanged cards, he opened the conversation with the following line: "What an award ceremony that was last night! Did you see the Oscars?"

I had arrived before arriving!

Chapter 39

# Ask Pertinent Que

A court jester in ancient India once asked t
treated the same as the prime minister. 
clever ploy to let the man discover the answ
asked the jester to get information about a
just set anchor. The jester rushed out an
that a foreign merchant vessel had indeed
him what merchandise the crew had brou
to the ship and returned with the answer. 
what did the captain of the ship want to 
and again the jester went in search of the a
back with it. After a few more suppleme
collapsed. Then the king asked the prim
port and find out about the ship, and the
complete information in one go. The jeste
minister had precedence in the court. 
story exist and they all teach the import
questions.

Ancient India was known for its trad

dialc
in o
trutl
thin
this
syste
a pr
dialc
doct
profe
use q
of qu

T
is ess
agen
of th
mana
tool f
als an
like tl

Tl
mana
jump
not th
react 
sustai
the ro
proble

To
until t

solution—only then is the solution sustainable. Quality experts maintain that when a problem occurs, by asking five consecutive "whys" you can usually uncover the root cause.

Here's a simple problem. An employee has been coming late to work for the last couple of days and the manager has to resolve the issue. A conversation ensues between the manager and the concerned employee.

Manager:   Why were you late today?

Employee: I missed the bus that normally brings me to work.

Manager:   Why did you miss the bus?

Employee: I woke up late.

Manager:   Why did you wake up late?

Employee: I went to bed late last night.

Manager:   Why did you go to bed late last night?

Employee: My wife has been suffering with viral fever for the last few days and I've had to attend to her.

The apparent reason here for the employee coming late is his missing the bus, but the root cause is that his wife has viral fever. Now consider if the manager had stopped at the first, second or even third "why." The potential conclusion and probable corrective action would have been vastly different! Though we need not stop at the fifth question to find the root cause and can go even deeper, the Japanese believe that most problems can be driven down to the root cause by asking "why" five times and then asking "how" just once.

Thus if the manager had asked the employee how his wife had contracted viral fever, the employee might have told him that they had gone out for a meal, after which she had come down with food poisoning, and the doctor had advised rest and a week's course of antibiotics. Now instead of forming a poor opinion of the worker's punctuality, the manager can adjust the employee's shift timings or give him some time off or simply wish his spouse a speedy recovery and not take any action against the employee.

A true professional, faced with a problem, will always question and find the root cause. Most people do not bother to get to that level. As a result they end up fixing the wrong set of problems.

The idea of professionalism dawned on me in 1990 when I visited the United States for the first time. I was in for a surprise when the hotel plumber came to my room. He was a big man in clean clothes. He wore a special belt around his waist from which hung at least two dozen tools of his trade. When he came, he did not attempt to fix the problem right away. He started by asking me questions, all kinds of questions, and then he asked me to simulate the problem. In many parts of the world, the plumber arrives without a tool kit. He jumps to fix the problem even before you have fully explained it, then tries to fix things with his bare hands, in the process floods the bathroom floor, and only then goes away to get the right tools and parts. And this is not only true of plumbers. It is the same with the cable TV installer, the auto mechanic, the carpenter and countless others up the value chain.

Consider this situation. Your washing machine is not working, and the repairman has come. First he opens the back of the machine, and black liquid pours out onto the bathroom floor. He looks lost. You have an uncomfortable feeling that the man does not know what he is doing.

But what if instead of jumping in to solve the problem, the

repairman began by asking pertinent questions: How old is the equipment? What is the exact nature of the problem? Has it ever happened before? He has come prepared with the right diagnostic tools, and explains to you the subsequent options, costs, parts needed and so on. Finally he asks you how long you can live without a functional washing machine, and then gives you a timeline for it to be fixed. Only then does he go about fixing it. And he closes by assuring you that if anything should go wrong, you can always contact him. He gives you a number to call. You do not call that number, but he calls you a week later to ask if all is well.

The professional competence of a nation is reflected in the way its plumbers, carpenters, auto mechanics and others engage with a problem and a customer. Without this no nation can become world-class even if it churns out neurosurgeons and software engineers.

While there is a clear, direct linkage between professional competence and the ability to ask pertinent questions, true professionals must also ask intuitive questions.

On one occasion I was asked to talk with someone in my organization who was going through a difficult professional patch. We knew each other well as colleagues and I assumed that we were comfortable enough with each other to discuss the details of his problems from the very outset. As we were sitting down for the meeting, I surprised myself by spontaneously asking, "Are you comfortable with me?" No sooner had I finished than my colleague blurted out that he was actually not comfortable. It was a crucial meeting, as the implications were huge, both for him and for MindTree. Without that one intuitive question, a polite conversation would have ensued and I would never have been able to get to the root of the problem or help him. What did I do when he expressed his discomfort? For a large part of the meeting, my job was not to discuss the core issue but to make him comfortable. The core issue could always be discussed, with greater clarity, but actually when he was comfortable.

While learning to ask pertinent questions is a basic skill, as we grow into positions of greater responsibility, it becomes necessary to refine that ability to the next higher level of critical questioning. I discuss critical questioning in Part Five and consider it a quality all professionals must strive to acquire. In the meantime, I'd like to address the corresponding ability to asking the right questions: the ability to listen intently.

Chapter 40

# Intent Listening

The pertinent, sometimes intuitive, questions need to be comple-
mented by intent listening. Listen to the answers to the questions
you have asked not only with your ears but also with your eyes.
Our eyes are trained to notice the smallest sign of pain, impatience,
lack of confidence, worry or detachment. Listen with your whole
body. Show engagement and signal through your eyes that at this
moment the only thing you care about is the person in front of
you. When you shift your eyes away from a person while listening
to her, it signals disengagement, distraction and lack of interest.

Listening is a physical function as much as it is an art. Some
people can see things others cannot. Much the same way, some
people can hear things others cannot. Good professionals are
invariably great listeners. The interesting thing about listening
is that the other person gets to "feel" instantaneously that he is
being listened to. As a result, a very positive energy starts flowing
between the two people who are in conversation. This positive
energy is often a prerequisite for diagnosis, problem solving and
collaboration.

The capacity to listen intently can be built with conscious practice.

A colleague sends an e-mail asking a question or raising an important matter. Immediately show interest by responding, not by mail but by calling the individual. During the call, suggest a personal meeting and fix the time on the spot rather than seeking an outlook meeting request. The listening process has already begun.

Now choose the right venue. I would not discuss a serious career issue in a restaurant because I do not want distractions of food or other people's conversations. We often pay little attention to choosing a venue appropriate to the mood of the other person, the intended subject of discussion and the desired outcome. But the right venue enhances listening.

Shut out distractions. In today's world we all pride ourselves on being multitaskers. But it is important not to have distractions like a television on in the background, a cell phone ringing or your BlackBerry in your hand and eyes darting toward it every once in a while.

Ask further questions as the conversation progresses, seek confirmation of your understanding, take notes if required, look for patterns in the information the other person is giving and relay the conversation back to him.

Intent listening reduces the time required for communication, makes the other person feel at ease and builds collaboration within and outside the organization. When we listen well, we signal empathy and engagement. This in turn helps build sound judgment. The world is starved for that one thing—each time you visit a dentist, a lawyer, an accountant, a banker or for that matter a mechanic, you wish they listened a little more!

# Chapter 41

# Human Beings First and Foremost

My mother had been lying motionless for forty-eight hours.

It all started the evening before when I returned from work and sat down to share my customary cup of tea with her. Susmita, my wife, called out to her to join us. Her frail frame refused to respond. She was breathing, softly, but she was not moving. It was clear this was an emergency. Luckily our family doctor came rushing over and asked us to move her to a hospital immediately.

It looked like she had had a stroke. The next forty-eight hours were critical, and all we could do was wait. At her advanced age, there was no question of an invasive procedure. As there was no internal bleeding, there was hope; the brain can recover magically.

My mother simply lay motionless on the hospital bed as we kept vigil. What was going on in her mind? Was there anything going on there at all? Could she hear us? Was she aware of her surroundings but could not speak? There was no knowing. Time was suspended in that hospital room.

The door opened and a young nurse walked in. She looked

about eighteen or nineteen. She probably got paid a tiny fraction of what professionals in the software industry get paid.

"*Ajji*," she said softly. *Ajji* in Kannada, the local language, means grandmother. "*Ajji*," she called again. I got up from the attendant's bed, startled and surprised that she was speaking to a person who had not spoken to anyone or moved in the last two days. What was she doing?

"*Ajji*, I am going to sponge you," she said.

Mother's body remained motionless.

"*Ajji*, I am going to make you sit up now." She changed my mother's position on the bed while gently supporting her with one hand.

Then she squeezed a wet towel and wiped my mother's face, her hair, her body, covering her at each step to maintain her modesty. All the time, she kept talking to her softly. Then she looked at me and asked me to leave the room because she had to change her. I went out in a daze. After ten minutes, the nurse came out and told me that I could go in. My mother lay motionless as before, but she looked like a freshly bathed child. The nurse had combed her matted hair, powdered her and left her looking content.

The day was long and monotonous. The only interruptions were when the same nurse returned, each time calling out, "*Ajji*, I need your temperature, I am going to open your mouth," "*Ajji*, I am changing the drip," "*Ajji*, I need to take your blood pressure."

That day it occurred to me that each time the nurse said "*Ajji*," she was placing my mother ahead of her work. For her my mother was a human being, not just a motionless patient in the hospital. My mother was a real person who needed her care.

·　　·　　·

Seeing the way that young nurse was treating my mother, my memory went back three decades to a hospital bed at a leading national medical research institution where I had been admitted with an undiagnosed high fever. While I was first treated for a viral infection and then suspected of typhoid, the fever raged, my body reduced to bones, hurting from the inside, burning outside. Susmita and I had just been married. My young wife was missing her university classes to be by my side. At times the pain was so intense I would bite Susmita's hand.

We were told that when the head of medicine made his rounds he would attend to my "case." It seemed we waited forever. Then, one morning, I realized there he was, looking down at me, with a group of interns and nurses surrounding him. Wearing a suit and a tie, he was the man. Right now, in his professionally qualified eyes, I was the "case." Someone showed him a sheaf of papers that hung from a metal clip tied to my bed. As I lay helpless, it seemed to me the case history clinically documented in those papers was a mysterious collusion between the doctors, the nurses and the gods. He briskly looked through the papers and then he spoke, in a clipped accent. "Young man," I heard him say, "you have tuberculosis. The good news is that it can be treated and you should become all right."

And then, in the very next moment, he and his convoy were moving on to the next bed. The man had just told me I had tuberculosis and simply walked away! I was completely devastated for the days that followed, until a diagnostic test established that I did not have tuberculosis and saved me from being put on medication.

· · ·

My mother recovered gradually and returned home. Years after, she passsed on. But the young girl who called her *Ajji* each time she came to attend to her needs has become an unforgettable part of me, a beacon of professionalism. The doctor who informed me I had tuberculosis is also unforgettable, but in contrast, as an enduring nightmare.

A professional must be empathetic, able to look at another person as a human being, to respect the other person no matter the state in which he or she appears—as a motionless patient, a demanding client or simply a harried customer. It is not enough to have the best skilled people on the job; they must respect life and living things.

Chapter 42

# The Rewards of Transparency

In 2008, MindTree won its single largest deal at the time against formidable global competition. The L. N. Mittal–led Mittal Steel had just bought out Arcelor, the largest steel conglomerate in Europe. Postacquisition, one of the tasks on hand for the new management was to improve cost, performance and profitability. As part of that overall strategy, they had decided to use offshore IT capability. At that time, MindTree had fewer than six thousand employees and did not really consider itself to be large enough and deep enough in terms of specific domain experience to meet the needs of ArcelorMittal. A steel company that size demands not only a large IT services company as a partner but also a very diverse set of capabilities, requiring both understanding of the steel industry as well as a multitude of software platforms.

When the bid papers did come to us, our European operations chief, Vishaal Gupta, studied them in detail. He realized that we did not have the full-spectrum capability to meet ArcelorMittal's needs. So he told ArcelorMittal that we were probably not their best choice based on our skill assessment and that we would participate only if we were allowed to make a partial bid. Their response surprised all of us.

ArcelorMittal said that we were the only company that had been honest enough to admit our limitations. They asked us to go ahead and put in our bid.

The next perceived hurdle was the future role of an existing vendor who had on-site presence, longtime entrenchment and knowledge of local conditions in ArcelorMittal's multiple European locations. We offered to take on the work but not as the prime vendor. We did not see it as being in the client's best interest to dislodge their existing relationship. We had value to add but not the capacity to replace the existing partner. ArcelorMittal did not reply. Instead, they sent a high-powered team to India for a detailed site visit. During a dinner we hosted for them, a call came from their corporate office informing us that, based on all the inputs they had, ArcelorMittal believed we could be the prime vendor with the existing organization as a subvendor, and if we were willing to take on that role, the business was ours.

Next thing we knew, we had a multiyear, multimillion-dollar relationship with ArcelorMittal. The genesis of that relationship was in Vishaal Gupta's ability to state clearly and up front what we were not capable of doing. Good clients value that because they know trust cannot be replaced by competence. Competence can be acquired, but trust either exists from day one or it does not. Knowing your individual limitations and the limitations of your company, telling a client, "No, we do not have the capability you require," is the professional thing to do.

# Chapter 43

# The Responsibility of Dissent

The word *satyam* in Sanskrit means truth.

On December 16, 2008, the sky above the Indian IT industry, which prided itself on its corporate governance, went dark. On this day, Satyam Computers, the country's fourth largest software exporter, had declared it would buy two companies owned by the chairman's sons for an astounding $1.6 billion. The chairman, Ramalinga Raju, and his family owned a meager 8.6 percent of the listed company. The two companies Satyam intended to buy were not only managed by Raju's own family members and largely owned by them, they were in the real estate business—an area that had absolutely nothing to do with the software business. On top of all this, the astounding valuation at which they were to be purchased was fictional. Satyam had decided that the land bank in the hands of the chairman's two sons, if constructed upon, was worth $1.6 billion. The entire board of directors, which consisted of several independent directors of international standing, simply agreed to a completely unrelated business acquisition with an interested party. Who were these men and women around the table who consented to one of the least transparent deals in Indian corporate history? What was on their minds when they raised their hands and said, "Aye"?

To answer this question, we must first look at the members of the board.

Dr. Mendu Rammohan Rao was dean and director of the Indian Institute of Management, Bangalore, prior to joining the Indian School of Business at Hyderabad as dean. He had also been a tenured professor in operations research at the famed Stern School of Business at New York University, served on several government boards and committees and won innumerable academic awards.

Dr. Krishna Palepu is a professor at Harvard University—specializing in strategy and governance! He teaches courses on making corporate boards and audit committees more effective and even co-led Harvard's Corporate Governance, Leadership and Values initiative.

Mangalam Srinivasan, arguably the lone dissenter since she was the first to take moral responsibility for the acquisition even though she did not really oppose the deal when it happened, is an adviser to the John F. Kennedy School of Government at Harvard.

Vinod Dham is a well-regarded Silicon Valley serial entrepreneur and investor who program-managed the Pentium chip at Intel and is considered a coinventor of flash memory. In addition, there was V. S. Raju, an ex-dean of IIT, Delhi, and T. R. Prasad, who served as cabinet secretary, India's senior-most bureaucrat, at one time.

Eminent people all, but they individually and collectively failed their shareholders, fifty-three thousand employees, families and their entire industry by their bizarre approval of the deal. While Mangalam Srinivasan was the first to step down in the wake of the scandal and admit to not having been vigilant enough or asking critical questions, Rammohan Rao defended himself in public, saying that the board had done no wrong in approving the deal.

In the following weeks, the company and the country went into convulsions as the Central Bureau of Investigation started unearthing murk in Satyam's financial dealings and revealed what it claimed to be a potential $3 billion fraud. Ramalinga Raju, his brother and the company's chief financial officer were put in jail and the board dissolved. *Business Line*, a leading financial newspaper, wrote on December 18, 2008, that the board did not have "a fig leaf of a cover."

As they sat down to consider the $1.6 billion deal, the Satyam board began their trip to Abilene.

The Abilene paradox is a management story in which a group of people agree to a course of action that is contrary to their individual preferences. The concept is attributed to Jerry B. Harvey, a management expert, and has since been captured in a film of the same name. The movie powerfully illustrates how people will agree to do strange things if they suppress their own voice and simply go along with what everyone else is saying. *The Abilene Paradox* should be seen by any professional who is part of any group that deliberates on issues of consequence.

The story begins one hot afternoon in Coleman, Texas, as a family is playing a game of dominoes. The father-in-law casually suggests that the family go to Abilene, a good fifty-three miles away, for dinner. The group concurs passively. The car ride is hell.

The food and service in the restaurant in Abilene are bad. On the way back, no one speaks. After they return, emotions erupt. Everyone points fingers at everyone else and disowns the idea of going to Abilene. Finally, when all fingers point to the father-in-law, he shrugs off responsibility by saying he never really wanted to go—he was simply testing the waters.

Every day, groups of professionals who work together take a trip to Abilene. That is how noncommittal agreements emerge and projects get kick-started. When things begin to fall apart, everyone blames everyone else for the decision and claims that he or she had simply gone along to avoid conflict.

The Satyam fraud was not limited to that one decision to buy out two family-run companies in a completely unrelated line of business for all the cash the company had. Nor was it one man's fault. No one—no matter how smart or cunning he is—can pull off something as gigantic as this, and all in one day.

I visited Satyam for the first time in 1996 when I was asked by Wipro chairman Azim Premji to go and see their campus under construction in Hyderabad. I was given a warm welcome. At the campus, I was served lunch, which turned out to be a dish of wild rabbit. That was rather unusual for an official lunch for a visitor, I thought. But I was told it was in my honor, as a special gesture. The rabbit had been shot on campus. Inside, I flinched, hoping the honor was not extended to visiting customers, some of whom could be animal rights activists.

Sometime afterward, I came across Satyam's annual report and balance sheet. It included the names of board members as is customary for any listed company. I was perplexed to see among them the name of a retired income tax official. What, I asked myself, was an ex-bureaucrat from the income tax department doing on the board of a software company?

Years later, I interviewed a Satyam consultant in Silicon Valley. He seemed like a good candidate for a job with us. After the interview, he surprised me by saying there was a component of his salary that was "unofficial."

It seemed that when Satyam had issued American Depository Receipts (ADRs) in the United States, a certain amount was reserved for employees as stock options. The candidate I was interviewing was unable to apply for them on time because of some official lapse. When the allocations were made, he lost out. He agitated about it, and the matter finally went to Ramalinga Raju. The chairman could not issue the ADRs to this employee for regulatory reasons. Instead, he said that each time the employee came to India for his annual vacation, the company would "unofficially" buy his family's tickets and that the arrangement need not be formally recorded.

While Raju was the entrepreneur behind Satyam, he was not its owner. In making many such decisions, he did not respect the difference between entrepreneurship and ownership. Mixing up the two ideas, he ran the company by fiat—sometimes malevolently, as in the case of the rabbit they shot for lunch, and sometimes benevolently, as with this employee enjoying the unaccounted perk.

But our focus in the Satyam fraud should not be on Ramalinga Raju. Our focus should be on the professionals around him who knew all along the company was taking one wrong step after another but chose to go along and earn their fat salaries and hefty bonuses. These people were failing the unwritten code of conduct for any professional—the responsibility of dissent.

Satyam is not the only organization where professionals fail to discharge their responsibility of dissent. It happens all the time and all around us wherever groups work together. When professionals meet, they often assume that the purpose of every meeting is to get consensus. But consensus is not always beneficial and can sometimes lead to disaster. This result can be avoided if each professional in a group exercises his responsibility of dissent and the purpose of the group's decision-making process is shifted from the urge to agree to the need to do the right thing.

From the power of vision to doing the right thing, individual decisions by professionals build the reputation an organization ultimately enjoys. The imperatives discussed in this section not only enable a professional to manage high volume, they also make good business sense. Outstanding companies recognize and actively incorporate them into their way of doing things, which then becomes corporate culture.

From managing volume, let us now shift to managing complexity. As a professional reaches the next higher plane, it is this ability that separates the best from the rest.

Part Five

# Managing
# Complexity

Chapter 44

# Three Disasters,
# Three Great Professionals

At eBay, an uninterrupted power supply is literally worth billions of dollars. The business of this California-based Internet auction site totally depends on its computers running 24/7 and, therefore, on the availability of power. And yet, ironically, there was a time when companies in California were more prepared for major disasters like earthquakes than for power outages. One day in 1999, all that changed. California suffered one of its worst power outages. The first outage lasted twenty-two hours. Power was restored briefly for eight hours, and then the second outage occurred. The power failure on that fateful day impacted every business in the region. When the servers unexpectedly went down, databases crashed, software programs went haywire and critical customer transactions were lost. All this meant lost money and reputation, and potential claims for damages.

At 5 P.M. on the day of the first outage, eBay CEO Meg Whitman got a call from her team estimating they could bring the site back up in a couple of hours once power was restored. Yet hours later it was still not up. Around midnight Whitman decided to go to her office and take charge of the crisis. For thirteen consecutive days she stayed right there, sleeping on a bed in the conference room, until business returned to normal. The fact that the CEO of eBay was there on-site twenty-four hours a day brought not only her entire organization together but also the best people from all the IT vendors whose collaboration was critical to repair the servers. She attended every single meeting—with the technical team and the marketing and finance teams—and it made a huge difference in their ability not only to get the site back up but to get it stabilized and confirm the integrity of the data. eBay was one of the first companies to recover from the outage and get its customers and business back.

At FedEx, time is money. How much money? Every minute's delay in turning around the planes that bring parcels to the company's hub in Memphis, Tennessee, costs FedEx a million dollars. In 1982, thirty-year-old Ken May was the managing director of what the company called Global Operations Control and Coordination (GOCC). One of the many tasks before his team was the deicing of aircraft in winter. Deicing preparedness obviously depends on the weather forecast. One night, Memphis was battered by an ice storm that moved in without warning and took Ken's entire setup by surprise—causing hours of delays and many millions of dollars in losses. Fred Smith, the CEO, asked for a postmortem. Explanations were sought and the place was abuzz with finger-pointing; the blame game had begun. Management author and Dartmouth professor Vijay Govindarajan recalls that when May walked into the room for the final conversation, there were signs of stress on everyone's face. And then Ken said that since he was the managing director of GOCC, the coordination of the deicing program was his responsibility. He said that he and his team had done a poor job that night and it was his fault. He took total responsibility for failure to execute. Ken had taken everyone by surprise, and the tone of the meeting shifted from witch-hunting and finger-pointing to how they could be prepared for such an event in the future.

The year 2001 will go down as the worst year in passenger airline history for a very obvious reason—the September 11th terrorist attacks in New York and Washington, D.C. The already ailing airline industry went into a tailspin after this. All airlines mothballed 20 percent of their planes, laid off 20 percent of their workforce and introduced across-the-board pay cuts. The only exception was Southwest Airlines, the low-cost leader of the U.S. airline industry.

Three days after 9/11, CEO Jim Parker and his leadership team had one monumental decision to make. The company was supposed to deposit $179 million into an employee profit sharing account, and everyone expected that Southwest would not make the payment. After all, who could tell what the future was going to be?

In what would appear to be a counterintuitive move, Parker decided "it was the right thing to do" and went ahead and made the payment. In addition, he decided Southwest would not ground planes or lay off any employees. As some flights ran below capacity, the company decided to let the excess staff handle customer calls for refunds as many passengers were wary of flying. To restore confidence, the airline announced a "no questions asked" refund for every cancellation. It went one step further by announcing more lower-fare deals in order to encourage people to fly again. Southwest made no salary cuts, except for board members and executive officers who volunteered to take them. The result? The company made a profit in the last quarter of 2001—a feat unsurpassed in aviation history—and its market cap was ahead of all other airlines combined.

When eBay CEO Meg Whitman decided to leave for her office on the night of the power outage and then stayed there for the next thirteen days, or when Ken May decided to own responsibility for the Memphis debacle, or when Jim Parker decided to do the right thing, what was going on in their minds? Were these decisions born of logical, rational thinking? What makes a professional think the way he or she does in a make-or-break situation? What is the source of the intelligence that guides such pivotal decisions? How do their minds actually "read" the big picture and yet focus on the small details at the same time? And more important, as we live in a world of unfolding complexity and unscripted events, what do professionals need to succeed in the future?

In the past, professionals like Whitman, May and Parker were told to make decisions based on data, facts and precedence. Other professionals who followed the same principle succeeded, and some did not. The future will be quite another story. As we look ahead, we need to get under the hood, to understand how the mind that makes critical choices in difficult moments works.

# Chapter 45

# Logic or Emotion?

One of the two oldest-known skeletons of an upright human is estimated at 4 million years old. It is what remains of a woman who is affectionately called Lucy by her keepers at New York's Museum of Natural History. Looking at her, we can safely conclude that we have been around in our current form for millions of years. And for the most part during our existence on the planet, the most prevalent human profession has been that of hunting. Radiocarbon tests indicate that only in the last 3,600 years have we known organized agriculture. So for millions of years we were hunters.

During the period when we were predominantly hunters, supporting professions rose up—the medicine man, the potter, the flint maker, the ironsmith. During the predominantly agricultural period, as civilizations evolved, newer professions came into being. In the last 400 years of the industrial and then the information economy, there has been an explosive growth in that number. But compared to a Wall Street dealer or a software engineer from Bangalore, professions during the hunting and farming phases of man's evolution had a longer sense of history; knowledge and skills were passed on from one generation to the next on a vastly large canvas of time.

In contrast, most modern-day professions have developed all too suddenly—in the course of a century at best. There is a far lesser sense of history to being a psychologist, a patent lawyer, a neurosurgeon, a dietitian, a television reporter or a software engineer. In that sense, we are still evolving and in some sense the so-called modern professional is really at the bottom of an evolutionary phase.

One significant difference between the modern professional and the hunter or farmer is probably the extent to which the former must use her brain. The brain as a tool has always been used, but its usage has varied dramatically among Lucy, her farmer descendants and her current-day service-sector progeny. This dramatic shift requires us to ask a very fundamental question: How well do we understand this tool which we use and rely upon as professionals? Do we know it as well as the hunter knew his spear and the farmer knows his plow?

The brain is our thought factory, and thought is the mother of all voluntary action. In the brain, billions of brain cells interact with one another to generate the thoughts, ideas and decisions that shape our activities and make us who we are. Until the 1980s, when magnetic resonance imaging (MRI) technology became available, there was little to no scientific understanding of how the brain works. In the last three decades, we have made tremendous progress; yet our current knowledge is probably just the starting point of an exploration that may possibly have no end.

Broadly speaking, the brain is divided into the left hemisphere and the right hemisphere. The left side controls the right side of the body and the right side controls the left. The left side is driven by logic, responsible for all analytical thinking; the right side thinks in terms of feelings, relationships and the big picture in any given situation.

Professions that emerged in the last hundred years emphasized analytical capability that largely requires left-brain thinking. This is the part of the brain that looks at everything in a causal sense; that is, for every cause there is an effect and for every effect there is a cause. It aids logic and problem solving. As we look back, we can see why the industrial economy that predominantly required left-brain thinking also saw the ascendance of accountants and engineers in the last century. During this time, modern science flourished. Modern management, as we know it, is an extension of modern science. As a result, logic has been the driving theme for most professionals over the past century.

Emotions, feelings, big-picture thinking and relationships were considered to be touchy-feely, not given easily to measurement and hence deemed outside mainstream management thinking. That paradigm is going to change in the decades to come. We are actually witnessing the emergence of a more balanced view in which emotions and feelings—attributes that determine creativity—are becoming as valued as logical thinking and analysis.

Daniel Pink, the author of *A Whole New Mind*, argues forcefully that right-brain thinking will actually dominate the future. It will help build differentiation in products and services we offer while factors like abundance, automation and Asia make everything into a commodity in every sphere of activity. He cites several powerful examples. Students of medicine at Columbia University are learning "narrative medicine," which goes beyond computer-based diagnostics and urges students to find the clue to the cure in the patient's story. Beyond the apparent illness, every patient has a story. Remember my lesson from Part Four. Often the difference between life and death is not technology, but how well the doctor "listens" to the story.

At the Yale School of Medicine students are honing their power of observation through courses at the Yale Center for British Art. When you look at a painting, you see the whole picture; you also see the details. A patient's face is no different from a painting. When a doctor examines a patient, the face can reveal a lot that could change the diagnosis. At UCLA Medical School, students are required to enact role plays pretending to be patients; they get admitted to hospitals so that these future doctors understand what it feels like to be at the receiving end. Ideas such as these originate in the right brain, which was largely allowed to hibernate in the twentieth century.

Remember my story about being diagnosed incorrectly with tuberculosis? While I lay listlessly on the hospital bed, waiting for the results from the tuberculosis test to arrive, Dr. Nabin Patnaik, an ophthalmologist, dropped by for a social visit. While talking to me, he noticed that my left eye was abnormally red. He "sensed" something was wrong and "intuitively" sought permission from the head of medicine to move me to the ophthalmic unit for a checkup. There, the tests revealed I had iritis, a condition in which the iris gets inflamed. Unchecked it could lead to a total loss of sight. My vision had actually dropped to 20/200 from a perfect 20/20. I was on my way to blindness and did not know it. The raging fever had taken my attention away from my failing eyesight, and I had not noticed I was steadily losing sight in one eye because

I was lying down all the time. What followed was a series of steroid injections on the eyeball and eventually I regained sight.

Why did the visitor notice something that scores of attending doctors and nurses had missed? What would have happened if I had recovered from the fever but lost my vision? What makes one person a better observer than another? Developing the right brain helps you look at the big picture, the context so to speak. When you see the big picture, you realize the interconnectedness of various facets of the problem. That is when you realize the problem is not what you thought it was, and hence the solution too cannot be what it has traditionally been. Unfortunately, in most countries, the educational system is designed to overfocus on the left brain at the cost of the right brain. As children, we are not encouraged to use the right brain; it then simply takes a backseat.

The professional in the twenty-first century must learn to use both sides of the brain, to harmonize both fact and feeling when making decisions. *A Whole New Mind* has a powerful illustration to drive the point home. In the book, there is a picture that shows the evolution of man—from ape to farmer, from farmer to blue-collar factory worker, to white-collar worker, and finally to a physician with a stethoscope around his neck, and, wait a minute, a paintbrush and palette in his hands.

This is the professional of the future—the master of facts and feelings.

# Chapter 46

# Multiple Intelligences

The brain's biggest gift to us is intelligence—it is our tool to learn, understand, explore and create. Just as we are only beginning to understand the brain itself, we are also only beginning to scratch the surface of "intelligence," which is the most important tool for any professional. What is the nature of intelligence? From the earlier discussion on what constitutes the left brain and the right brain, we looked at how the twentieth century saw the emergence and the somewhat misplaced priority accorded to the left brain. Not surprisingly, the idea of intelligence was also equated with left-brain activity, which is mathematical-logical in nature. In effect, this became the basis of intelligence and its measure is known as intelligence quotient or IQ.

The real story behind IQ is recounted in Harvard professor Howard Gardner's pathbreaking work *Multiple Intelligences*. It was the year 1900. The city of Paris was witnessing a huge influx of villagers who migrated along with their children. In the preceding year, France had made it mandatory for all children between the ages of six and fourteen to attend school. So the law required that no child in that age group be left behind. Suddenly, the pressure on the Parisian school system became huge. In order to cope with the influx, the authorities needed a way to assess the intelligence of children so that the more intelligent among them got priority. They turned to a self-taught psychologist named Alfred Binet, who devised a method that has come to be known famously as the IQ test. At the time, it was largely a test of mathematical-logical capability in an individual. The idea of the IQ test as we understand it today has its roots here. Later, the U.S. Army became its largest user during drafts for the world wars.

Howard Gardner's work brought the limited nature of mathematical-logical capability—and the mistake we make when we equate it with intelligence—to the attention of people the world over. His book lists eight other forms of intelligence to illustrate the point. These are: literary, musical, kinesthetic, interpersonal, intrapersonal, spatial, naturalistic and, finally, spiritual. Professionals must be aware of each of these intelligences to harness the brain, to think, to ideate, to innovate and solve problems. It is important to understand them and how each one works, because in varying degrees we are all gifted with all nine intelligences to deliver better results and enjoy life more.

Literary intelligence is about the capability to read and write as much as imagine. Today, between a chief executive who can do the math and another who also reads extensively and writes some, the latter would succeed many times over. In a world in which we have to network and collaborate with dispersed teams, some in faraway lands and time zones, the capacity to build leadership proximity is determined by how well you express yourself through language. Developing excellent language skills for any professional then is extremely important.

When I was growing up, music or music appreciation was not a usual part of school or college curricula. It was considered "feminine" to pursue such activities; boys were encouraged to play sports, not learn music and dance. Music is about harmony. Studies indicate that children who play an instrument learn to listen much better—they grow up to be empathetic professionals. Not everyone is endowed with the intelligence to write lyrics, compose, perform or play an instrument, but the capacity to build appreciation can be cultivated by anyone, and it has several benefits beyond just entertainment.

Great athletes have what is called kinesthetic intelligence. In certain kinds of sports, you do not have time to think. In fact, thinking actually sets you up for failure. Consider boxing, fencing, soccer or even baseball. When you see a baseball player like the Yankees' Alex Rodriguez at bat, you realize that he has intelligence in his muscles and learning ability in his hands and legs. Even when a ball is coming at him at ninety miles per hour, he can decide whether to swing and how based on the spin and arc of the ball. Such people are able to make critical decisions involving the body and the mind on the fly, where each move is a new move. For some, life depends on this ability. How is a firefighter, a policeman or a trauma surgeon's job any different? How much time do you think they have to process information and take action in an emergency? Increasingly, professions of the future will need leaders with greater kinesthetic capability to reduce the gap between sense and response.

You must have come across many people who are naturally able to converse, make friends quickly, read other people's emotions or solve difficult problems collaboratively. These people have a higher degree of interpersonal intelligence. They build more empathy and can work better as part of a group. This is hugely important for people who want to lead. In the future, the ideas of leadership, followership and situational collaboration will be extremely important. Sometimes you lead, at other times you follow, but at all times you have to collaborate—and a professional of the future has to be able to collaborate effectively.

Given a position of power and authority, why does one person behave in a despotic manner and another in a humane way? The former is not self-aware, the latter is. Some people are more self-aware than others. Yet everyone has the capacity to build self-awareness. In my work with young leaders, I find that those who are more self-aware have a realistic understanding of who they are and what their true needs are. As a result, they are emotionally more stable and can deal with the ups and downs in life and work far better than others. These people have a higher degree of what Gardner calls intrapersonal intelligence. This is extremely important in professionals whose decisions affect a large number of other people.

Spatial intelligence gives us navigational capacity. In the days of yore, some seafarers were specially chosen for their navigational skills. On an overcast night, they could steer a ship and instinctively know true north. In today's world, in a profession like sales, some salespeople can map and chart a client organization much better than others. Some people can land in an alien town and map it so well that they become demonstrably more productive than others. I suspect these are more spatially intelligent people.

In our hunting and farming days, every tribe had someone who was better at recognizing animal calls or could tell one animal from another by looking at hoof prints or pugmarks. That individual was very important for the safety of the hunters and the success of their mission. When farming dominated human activity, this person was the one who knew one herb from another, could tell you which wild mushroom to eat and which one would kill you. He was the one gifted with naturalistic intelligence. As we all become more environmentally aware and sensitive to the planet, naturalistic intelligence, that is, the ability to relate to the natural world, will be much more in demand across professions.

Finally there is what Gardner calls spiritual or existential intelligence. We are all hardwired to appreciate the presence of a higher power. Some people can connect more easily with the spiritual world and as a result they can better deflect anxiety, can better deal with loss, and can better balance decisions with yardsticks of morality and self-governance. Such professionals, who know and can do the right thing the right way, will increasingly become relevant in the world of business.

Chapter 47

# Three Levels of Knowledge

All professionals work with bodies of knowledge within a certain domain. And all things being equal, different individuals relate to the same body of knowledge within that given domain very differently and with astonishingly different outcome possibilities. According to Yves Doz, a professor at INSEAD, France, people relate to knowledge at three different levels.

At the lowest level, we relate to knowledge in a technical context. At this level, knowledge is all about specifications handed down to a professional who needs to create something. It is the kind of knowledge required for reverse engineering. Someone shows me an object or a model and I build a similar artifact with the desired form and functionality. I do not question, I do not add substantial new value. This is also called the adaptive layer. There is no innovation involved at this level. A professional who works at this level is unlikely to be differentiated and, in reality, as the world changes, could become extinct one day.

At the next higher level is the experiential layer of knowledge. This level is not about technical specifications and the functionality of the product or service we make or offer. Here the professional gets into the shoes of the end user, building a product or creating a service based on the experience of the target customer. When Nissan wanted to design a car for the European market, their engineers did not merely take a Japanese engine and create a body with European styling. Instead, Nissan sent a delegation of auto designers to Europe. When they got off the plane, each rented different makes of cars and drove thousands of miles all over Europe to understand what it meant to be a motorist there. They imbibed the motoring experience in the French Alps, the Italian countryside, the German autobahn—all vastly different from one another. Then they came back and designed a car that was right for the European driver. They created a product after they understood the consumer experience.

Beyond these two levels is the existential layer of knowledge where it is not about getting into the shoes of the customer but about "creeping into the minds" of customers. When Sony designed the Walkman, it was operating at this level. Sony is Sony not because it manages five thousand different products, or because it knows ferrite magnet technology, DSP chips and liquid crystal displays better, or because it builds more competitive and more optimal supply chains. What differentiates Sony is the fact that its designers understand what goes on inside the heads of its customers. For example, they have a feel for what happens to a kid in the Bronx when he dons his headphones, hits the play button and begins to wriggle in tune with his favorite music. The professionals at Sony work backward from that feeling to design innovative products and services.

Individual professional progression charts a very similar path. The best professionals operate at the existential level where it is about building the capacity to engage with people, problems, processes and opportunities by creeping into the minds of customers. This requires empathy, inclusion, 360-degree thinking, recognizing the interconnected nature of things, looking for solutions outside the box, learning from unusual sources and finally cutting through complexity and doing so with empathy.

A professional I have deep admiration for is the internationally renowned cardiac surgeon Dr. Devi Shetty. When you visit his famous hospital, Narayana Hrudayalaya in Bangalore, you first encounter a small shrine in front of the portico. It is a small, four-cornered structure. One side is a temple, the other a church, the third side is a mosque and the fourth a *gurdwara* (a place of worship for Sikhs). The doctors at Narayana Hrudayalaya will tell you this shrine is where all healing begins—from faith and then on through the hands of the doctor. Beyond the portico, as you step inside the building, is a well-organized reception area, which has a sign in Bengali that says "BENGALI SPOKEN HERE." In Bangalore, almost everyone speaks either English or Hindi or both. Why does the hospital require a separate area within reception for patients who are more comfortable speaking Bengali? Because demographic analysis of patients has shown that most heart patients who come to the hospital are from West Bengal in India and neighboring Bangladesh and are often escorted by a fellow villager, spouse or family member for whom an alien city, a hospital and the burden of an unknown language can be daunting. Dr. Shetty has created his institution based on existential knowledge, on understanding how a patient who visits his hospital feels.

At the end of a long day, Dr. Shetty sits in his office and sees outpatients. He always tries to say a few words to each patient in their mother tongue. Sometimes his accent is clumsy, but his gesture instantly endears him to them and makes them feel at ease. He uses his stethoscope to examine them, something that is probably meaningless in a clinical sense because he has their entire case history, including CT scans, in front of him. But he does it because most patients from rural areas feel a doctor has not paid attention to them or examined them thoroughly unless he has listened to their heartbeat with a stethoscope. And, invariably, he will touch them at least once during the conversation. When I asked him why he did that, he told me that these days doctors do not understand the power of the human touch. There can be no healing without touch. After he has examined the patient, a completely unhurried Dr. Shetty ends the consultation by asking, "Do you want to ask me anything?" For a man strapped for time this can be risky, because patients may engage him in a long conversation. But for Dr. Shetty this is the most important thing to do.

Dr. Shetty relates to the world of medicine at the existential level. And this is what will be required of every world-class professional of tomorrow—be it a dress designer, product manager at Procter & Gamble, a physician, a family attorney or an air traffic controller.

Chapter 48

# The Five Minds of the Future

Our brain is the repository of nine intelligences. The mind, which is the abstract layer of the brain, works with these nine intelligences. Howard Gardner tells us we have more than one form of intelligence and in reality more than one mind. We can be masters of many minds by using our multiple intelligences. It is in this context that he writes about the "five minds of the future." These are: the mind of discipline, the mind of synthesis, the mind of creativity, the respectful mind and the ethical mind. To illustrate the five, I often ask audiences to simulate a situation.

Imagine you are the police chief of your city. You get a phone call from the governor of your state informing you that in an hour's time a hijacked plane will land at the city airport. You have to take charge. What are you going to do? What decisions are you going to make? And how are you going to make those decisions?

It is amazing how groups can spend hours discussing what needs to get done even though in a real hijacking situation, there is generally no time to discuss.

You need to rush to the airport, of course. You need to gather all intelligence reports and get a well-briefed police force in there. But you also need commandos who are better trained to handle terrorists. While the police can handle the outer perimeter of the airport, it is the trained commando who must handle the plane and the hijackers. You need a trained hostage negotiator. You probably need a language interpreter (the terrorists may not be conversant in your language). You need aviation experts. You need doctors—first-aid experts, specialists who deal with trauma victims, a cardiac specialist and a burn injury specialist just in case. You need paramedics. You need food and water. You need fire engines and fire experts. You need the bomb disposal squad. You need forensic experts and body bags and DNA fingerprinting capability. You need trained communicators because you will need to talk to many different stakeholders and not just the media. Above all, as the police chief who has an hour to put preparedness in place, you need the five minds of the future.

First and foremost you need the mind of discipline, which means your own discipline as a police officer. You must be a master of all the things needed to run the police force. Studies done at Harvard and Stanford universities indicate that mastering any discipline takes as long as ten years. To be a good surgeon, a good photographer, a good teacher or a good software engineer, it is not enough to be technically qualified or professionally educated; you need sustained, devoted practice over years to truly know the nuances of your discipline, understand the big picture, the dependencies and the domain.

But knowing how the police force works is just one small part. Mission success now depends on knowing how other disciplines work as well. All professional problems of the future will require an interdisciplinary approach. Thus the police chief needs to know the workings of aviation experts, the antihijack squad, doctors, psychologists, etc. Should he make the decision to storm the plane or negotiate and psychologically wear down the hijackers? This calls for the capacity to synthesize information from many different disciplines. This is where you will need the mind of synthesis—the capacity to look at any issue, any solution from a multidisciplinary viewpoint.

Because life is going to throw at us increasingly unscripted problems—like the hijack drama unfolding before us—we need to build the creative mind. Solutions in life cannot always be resource intensive; sometimes the best solutions are found on the fly, using available resources. Until the trained interpreter arrives, the air traffic controller may be a better bet to keep the hijacker engaged. Persuading the hijacker to let a multilingual nurse on board help with a woman in labor while waiting for a gynecologist may be the smarter thing to do; asking the local army hospital to send a gynecologist may be even better than sending for a civilian doctor. Now you begin to see how almost all steps, thousands of them, through the hijack crisis need to be extremely creatively thought out and how each decision has downstream consequences, like a game of chess.

The police chief cannot handle the problem on his own. He requires the fire chief, the chief medical officer, the head of public relations, army and aviation experts, to name a few collaborators he must rely on. Now we have a different dimension to the problem. These people are experts (not amateurs) in their own disciplines. There are potential problems dealing with experts—they are all extremely knowledgeable in their respective fields, and they can be egotistical people who do not necessarily get along with other experts. So in a situation such as we have, we need a police chief who has a respectful mind. Only a person who knows how to iron out differences, bring out the best in other people, get consensus and buy-in for difficult options—all in the shortest possible time with the fewest possible unwanted consequences—is a true professional of the future. Leaders in every profession must learn to deal with others with respect. In the situation we are discussing, that one capacity may make the difference between large-scale destruction and a negotiated settlement that saves innocent lives.

Finally, every great professional requires what Gardner calls the ethical mind. To me, the ethical mind is not just a morally sound mind. Should the police chief pay a ransom or not? Is it better to concede to the hijackers' demands to save the babies on board? Professionals must begin with the basics. Being a professional will also mean understanding the larger implications of our decisions and our processes, and deriving our actions from a higher code of conduct—that of self-regulation and belief in the practice of fair dealing in every transaction.

# Chapter 49

# Critical Questioning

The true professional has the capacity to raise incisive, difficult and sometimes uncomfortable questions that become potential game changers. Such questions can be inherently counterintuitive and often differ from collective wisdom. Critical questioning is a powerful tool available to every professional. However, it requires understanding and then cultivation. As you sharpen the power of critical questioning, you begin to ask the right questions. This opens up many possible solutions beyond what is apparent on the surface.

Michael Marquardt, author of *Leading with Questions*, talks about how people refrain from asking questions because they do not want to rock the boat, risk looking foolish or interrupt the "harmony" of an organization.

The *Titanic* sank on her maiden voyage from England to the United States in April 1912. More than 1,500 people died. Some of the people who had designed or been involved in building the ship had serious doubts about her design, but they kept quiet as she sailed because they did not want to look foolish in front of the majority of their colleagues who did not seem to share their doubts. Even as she was undertaking the crossing, it seems other ships in the vicinity had radioed the *Titanic* warning her of icebergs. But those on the ship ignored the warnings. Read: Someone did not exercise the professional requirement to raise critical questions about how the presence of icebergs might affect the ship. Someone did not agitate enough. What followed was one of the worst maritime disasters in history.

In 1961, President John F. Kennedy gave clearance for a covert attack on Cuba by 1,400 Cuban exiles in what has been termed the Bay of Pigs disaster. Intelligence reports indicated that such an attack would unleash a popular uprising in Cuba resulting ultimately in the overthrow of Fidel Castro. Contrary to expectations, when the 1,400 exiles landed, they were far outnumbered by the Cuban military, which was forewarned of the assault. More than a thousand were taken prisoner and hundreds died. One key assumption when making this decision was that the exiles would scatter into Cuba—how they would do this when between the Bay of Pigs and the mainland lay eighty miles of swampland remains unclear. Was the question ever asked? When the mission failed, it was apparent that the president had been misled and it was even clearer that people who had doubted the success of the strategy had suppressed their urge to question it because everyone else seemed to be so gung-ho on the idea.

After the Bay of Pigs fiasco, "groupthink" as a concept emerged and was researched extensively by celebrated Yale psychologist Irving Janis in the 1970s. Janis brought to light how groups of decision makers become blind to impending warnings when they are bound together on a mission and how group members fail to raise critical questions because of the need for false harmony.

When we ask critical questions, we begin to understand the interconnected nature of things. In other words, we are able to build a larger, systemic view.

Peter Senge at MIT uses an interesting example—that of highway congestion—to explain this. In Senge's scenario, traffic planners decided that the best way to ease congestion on a busy road in a city was to add another lane. After the lane was created, the congestion worsened despite the fact that traffic volume had not increased. What was the reason? The availability of the additional lane had actually encouraged drivers to change lanes more frequently, hoping that they could get to their destinations faster. When everyone tried to do that, the result was chaotic driving and worse congestion.

The inadequacy of the well-intended measure was caused by nonexploration of systemic issues—that is, not exploring all aspects that cause traffic snarls, including bad driving, an effect of human psychology that involves opportunity seeking, risk taking and a host of other factors that make drivers as much a problem as the width of the road.

This is not to say that the road widening was not needed. It is to suggest that other factors needed to be unearthed by asking the right set of questions. These could have been remedial measures like teaching drivers to follow lane discipline, allocating the new lane for only certain categories of vehicles at certain times or simply allowing one lane on the reverse side of the road for traffic to move in the opposite direction during peak hours.

• • •

There are stories galore in management literature that tell us how the predominant role of a CEO is to ask questions, not give the answers. Jack Welch, one of the most admired CEOs of the twentieth century, was famous for asking questions and using them to build a high-performance culture among his leaders. In the process, he helped build one of the most valuable companies in the world: General Electric. GE is an extremely diversified company, with activities ranging from financial services to aircraft engines, medical equipment to plastics and domestic appliances. The company could well be a CEO's nightmare to manage.

Jack Welch knew the power of questions. In managing and uniting GE's very diverse businesses, he would invariably ask himself a set of five specific questions about the leader of each of the various businesses.

- Is he real?
- Does he see around the corners?
- Who's around him?
- Does he get back on the horse?
- Is he pro-business?

Welch's penchant for asking questions as a way of simplifying complex issues extended to areas beyond business as well. In a much talked-about article he wrote in *The New York Times* on October 30, 2004, to help Americans choose a new president, he asked voters to ask themselves these same five questions when evaluating the candidates.

Through these five questions, Welch brought out five important leadership imperatives of the U.S. president: authenticity, capacity to see the big picture, ability to attract and surround oneself with competent people, capability to recover from mistakes and the ability to see business as a driver for nation building.

Welch was not the first to understand the power of questions as a professional requirement. In the 1970s, Motorola Corporation embraced the idea of Total Quality Management (TQM). The company not only won the Malcolm Baldrige Award, considered the Nobel Prize of quality management in the United States, but used the idea of TQM to completely reinvent itself. Motorola used Six Sigma—a TQM adaptation—and following Motorola, companies like Allied Signal, GE and many more began to apply Six Sigma principles. The concept of Six Sigma quality can be very complex and sometimes difficult to understand for people without some knowledge of statistics. To ensure that everyone in the organization embraced Six Sigma, Motorola used a framework of building questions that could help even the mathematically challenged understand the idea of quality at some basic level and build an action plan for continuous improvement. Toward this end, everyone in the company was required to answer the following questions:

- What is my product or service?
- Who is the customer for my product or service?
- What do I need to do to deliver my product or service?
- What are the Critical to Quality (CTQ) requirements of my customers?
- What is my "As-Is" condition?

- How do I Define, Measure, Analyze, Improve and Control?

When people start seeing their work as an output on which someone else depends, they start recognizing the other person as a customer. They begin to realize their dependence on others to create their product or service. Once they see their recipient of the output as a customer, they learn to go and seek out the voice of the customer. This becomes the CTQ requirements without which the product or service falls short of gaining the customer's approval. They learn to measure the current level of quality vis-à-vis what the customer needs and thereby create a process for continuous improvement.

But it all starts with the idea of critical questioning. Critical questioning is the starting point for every quality journey. And that includes the journey toward personal quality as well.

Chapter 50

# Dealing with Personal Pain

In our jobs, particularly at senior positions, each of us deals with a host of complex situations and difficult problems every day. These help all of us to grow as managers and leaders. At the same time they also build pressure, and before you know it, you are in your forties, and have to face many challenges on the personal front as well. It could be your own health, an aging parent diagnosed with a terminal illness, perhaps marital discord that ends in separation, or problems associated with raising teenage children. These are life-changing events that are bound to affect anyone. How you manage yourself and sometimes deal with personal tragedy determines how you will grow as a professional in the years ahead.

One of the most uplifting stories of someone dealing with personal pain while in the line of fire is that of Anu Aga, former chairman of Thermax. Anu took on the mantle of chairmanship after her husband died suddenly in 1996. She had no time to mourn. The board asked her to step in and take charge of the company her father had started and her husband had built as a nationally reputed engineering organization. She took over the reins within forty-eight hours of her husband's death. Barely a year later and within a fortnight of one another, her mother-in-law, her pet and her son died. Her son died in a road accident while driving back from Bangalore to Pune after personally fixing the problem of a dissatisfied customer. Anu balanced herself through all this and remained steadfast. Under her leadership, the company grew, and she reconstituted the board, divested unrelated businesses and improved performance several fold. In 2004, she handed over the reins of the company to her daughter Meher Pudumjee.

Dealing with personal pain can have a debilitating impact on one's work and that is understandable. Yet somewhere we must draw the line so that the deeply personal does not override duty. Surprisingly, a personal crisis can also bring focus and attention to one's job, helping us achieve higher and better standards. In many ways, it sometimes transforms us as professionals.

Faced with a personal setback, the first thing a professional must do is to secure his or her professional position. Your commitment to your job and to performing to the best of your capabilities cannot be compromised. It makes no sense to let a personal tragedy submerge the platform that provides us with the power of continuance. Allowing personal issues to drown professional obligations is like abandoning the shelter before the storm has passed.

If a personal problem is beginning to overwhelm you, inform your organization. Seek help in reprioritizing your work on hand so that deadlines and commitments do not fall between the cracks. If required, take time off. The period of adjustment varies depending on what you are up against. Renegotiate your contract, work hours and compensation until you feel stronger. The key is to plan, strategize, know the trade-offs, build backups and keep people informed. Most professional and progressive workplaces understand this and find creative ways to help a valuable individual cope with a period of stress. Return to full-time responsibilities only when you feel you can once again give your best to your organization. And come back with full force.

Part Six

# New World
# Imperatives

Chapter 51

# Rainmaking

---

I have spent the last several chapters discussing the importance of managing volume and managing complexity. But in today's increasingly fast-paced and competitive world, it is not enough to simply manage what you have been given; you must also seek to create new opportunities for yourself and your business. You must see yourself as a rainmaker.

The term "rainmaker" was first used by Native Americans to connote a medicine man who by various rituals and incantations sought to literally make it rain. Today, the term implies an organizational man (or woman) with an exceptional ability to attract clients, leverage the network, amplify the brand values and increase profits. In short, a rainmaker is a professional with disproportionate capacity to add value to the organization. This ability has become a fundamental requirement for all CXO positions in any organization.

Rainmaking is often associated with the act of selling. We are all familiar with stories of the sales guy who, upon finding no leads in a territory or an account, consciously skips it and begs to be shifted to a better ground. Then, when another salesperson is assigned to the same territory, she is miraculously able to win business and make deals on the same barren land! Managers love her, and the entire organization looks up to her, but no one really knows how she does it. She is a rainmaker.

But rainmaking is not about selling alone. To be a true rainmaker, one must rise above anonymity in every function and become a critical asset in every organization.

Imagine an editor of a publishing house who is not just good at her job but has a knack for picking up best-selling authors. That individual is a rainmaker without being a salesman. Or for that matter, take a chief technology officer at a high-tech Silicon Valley company who is an inveterate geek but has the special capability to anticipate trends in technology, which allows his company to gain a competitive edge and raises the bar for the entire industry. Think of a surgeon who actively cultivates industry contacts and is visible at various platforms. As a result, she gets favorable press that helps her hospital stay ahead of the competition. In the process, the hospital is chosen to receive government funding for research in a new area, leaving its competition behind. In each case, the professional involved is not just doing a first-rate job in his or her own specialized area but also actively seeking opportunities to expand the organization's revenue, profitability, reputation and overall impact. The professional is personally enhancing the organizational brand value. She is a living logo.

It is important to remember that rainmakers were not born with any sort of special ability. Rather, they cultivated their skills with conscious effort and over a long period of time. They recognized rainmaking as a professional requirement that would allow them to make a larger impact. When you observe such people closely, you can discern a set of practices they do almost effortlessly. But as I said, developing this talent begins with recognizing that it is a matter of priority, an important deliverable for anyone in a position of consequence in the organization. At the core of that recognition is respect for the larger goals of the organization. You cannot be head of R&D or production or supply chain or HR and not recognize the value of improved sales, profitability or other things that affect the competitiveness and leadership of the overall system. This means, in some sense, we are all salesmen and -women. In today's hypercompetitive world, selling is not an option at a senior level. Someone sells the product or service to an end customer; others sell the brand, the image, the technology prowess, employment and the financial transparency of the organization to stakeholders. That said, people are seldom trained for it.

I have met Bill Gates only once. He was visiting India in the year 2000 and my boss was invited to be part of a small group of industry leaders to listen to him. My boss could not attend and so sent me. I was very flattered and flew in all the way to Delhi from Bangalore hoping that the man would enlighten me about the future of future. When Gates appeared and took the podium, he spoke evangelically about something I felt to be quite devastating. He spoke about how Microsoft Windows would change the world. My first reaction was disbelief, replaced by disappointment. As I returned to Bangalore, suddenly it dawned on me why Bill Gates was selling Windows. After all, what else did he have? And if he did not sell Windows, how on earth could he expect his field force to believe in it? Bill Gates believed his number-one job was to sell Microsoft and its products. Anything esoteric fills his ego but not his coffers. That is the reason why Microsoft is where it is today, despite what detractors may say of it. Whether it is Jeff Immelt of GE, Larry Ellison of Oracle, Richard Branson of Virgin or Indra Nooyi of PepsiCo, today's successful CEO is focused on his or her company's revenue and reputation. He uses important platforms and connections, goes along to make a sales call or join in for a closing. These initiatives give him a firsthand customer perspective as well as providing the sales organization with the motivation to do a better job. Today's CEO is a rainmaker. People who aspire to larger responsibilities better master the art of rain-making well in advance and certainly before the organizational line-up to pick the chosen one.

Rainmakers are constantly searching for opportunities to pass on to their sales organizations any knowledge they gain through contacts, competitor information, reading, trade shows, meetings and networking. "Who is doing what?" and "Who is saying what?" are often critical pieces of organizational knowledge that can only be acquired through the eyes and ears of a seasoned professional. Thus attending industry events and trade shows results in important learning points for any organization, and it is not just the sales personnel who need to go. Sometimes, the most valuable leads are generated not by salespeople, but by employees in other departments who must train to spot and seize opportunities.

There are a few other aspects of rainmaking that all of us should know about.

A rainmaker is invariably a good spokesperson. He is able to articulate statements on behalf of his organization to the outside world. Sometimes all of us need to present a point of view to the trade press; sometimes we are called upon to make a presentation to a trade body or a financial analyst. In a world of global business, we all have to play host to an overseas delegation every now and then. Chances are, in addition to making a presentation on your organization, you will have to answer a barrage of questions: on your organization, on the industry and, quite often, on your country's policy issues. A lot of people fumble through such occasions. Few organizations train their senior professionals to be spokespeople, but it is not that hard to learn. It is different from public speaking and simply making good presentations. It involves articulating a point of view on a subject of importance, and sometimes handling questions on difficult issues, particularly in difficult times. Public relations agencies are usually a good resource to get trained in how to become an effective spokesperson. Effective spokespersonship requires understanding of how different media work. I always considered myself to be a reasonably good presenter but was not aware of how to handle television interviews. I used to be long-winded whenever a question was thrown at me. My trainer taught me a simple thing. "Publish the headline first," he would say. When we read the newspaper, we do not begin with the body copy first. Imagine having to read through an entire article just to find out what the story is all about. Instead, I was told, one must speak in short sentences, provide the position on the subject as a headline of sorts and then allow follow-up questions to get deeper into the subject. During the conversation, one needs to use data, illustrations and examples to leave memorable key points. But the hook is always the headline.

In today's world, every professional has to frequently attend video- and teleconferences, which present their own nuances. Speaking to a live audience is vastly different from speaking to someone halfway across the world, even if you can see them, and it is much more difficult to engage people this way. The ability to have a conversation in a remote mode, sometimes with people you do not know, can be very daunting. All of us must learn phone, video and Web skills; these are no longer a nice-to-have capability.

Rainmakers understand and stay current with their organization's key business parameters and the issues concerning them in the environment; they scout for opportunities for new business, sometimes an unusual source of supply, an alliance that expands operations to a hitherto new area, and they attract high-quality talent. These require a professional to learn how to speak the language of the business he or she belongs to, and it begins with the ability to make an engaging presentation on what their organization does. It is amazing how few people realize the importance of something as basic as this. If you cannot make a good presentation of your organization, you will never be able to speak confidently and clearly about issues at an industry level.

Last but not least, as we all progress to positions of seniority in any field, we need to understand that we can no longer live off the organization's brand. In fact, the brand of any organization is an aggregation of the personal brand of its top team. Thus building a personal brand and making it visible are important professional requirements for everyone. My personal brand is all about what I stand for. What are my key beliefs and positions on important issues? This is something that gets built over time through what you say in public forums, what views you propagate, what organizations you endorse and what you write in newspapers, magazines and blogs. My cofounder at MindTree, Kalyan Banerjee, tells young leaders to frequently check their "Google Quotient." If someone makes a Google search on your name, what is likely to show up? If the answer is nothing or nothing substantive from an organizational point of view, then you are probably not a rainmaker yet.

Rainmakers are invariably visible in what I term "alternative spaces." These are your organization's Web site, your personal blog, YouTube, Facebook and such other places on the Internet where people may look for you before contacting your organization. What they find about you will help shape their first impressions about your organization. Take for instance Steve Jobs of Apple. The commencement speech he delivered at Stanford University is on YouTube and it has been viewed more than 600,000 times! In it, you not only learn about life lessons from the man who founded Apple, but by listening to him speak, you build an opinion about Apple itself. How much did Apple have to spend on creating the video, posting it on YouTube and keeping it there? Not a dime. The value of that one video is worth millions of dollars of paid advertising. That is the power of rainmaking.

# Chapter 52

# Inclusion and Gender

In 1998, Susmita and I decided to build our own house. We bought a piece of land, but we needed to take out a home loan so we could start construction. We went to a leading private sector bank in India to discuss the loan. Sitting in front of the manager, I told him off the bat that although I would be the borrower on record, it was really my wife who managed all our finances and made all the financial decisions, and she had some questions to ask before we made up our minds. But as Susmita began to ask the relevant questions, the manager would steadfastly ignore her and look at me while answering. It was clear that he did not consider her important. In the end, despite the bank's marginally lower rate of interest, we decided to take a loan from another bank. It was clear that the first bank would not treat Susmita on par with a man. This was a practical problem since I would not have been able to accompany Susmita to all meetings with the banker. She would be dealing with him on an ongoing basis, and she would obviously not have been taken seriously.

Countless people unconsciously discriminate against women

in everyday work life. A man is assumed to be more competent, more technically savvy than a woman, and some men still believe that a female colleague is someone to be accommodated, not accepted or treated as an equal. Despite an increasing number of women at the workplace and in positions of power, in the average workplace transaction we remain very male-centric. Going forward, professionals have to be more aware of gender issues while dealing with colleagues, customers and suppliers.

When a group of fellow workers go out for lunch and there is a lone woman in the group, without realizing it, the men begin to engage with one another and usually the woman is expected to blend in. Some people believe that it is the woman's responsibility to do so; men do not realize how quickly they actually create a fortress of sorts that shuts women out. By virtue of being a woman it becomes difficult to be part of the group, even though the person to be included is a coworker, not an outsider. It is a silent problem in every workplace.

Many may think that in a developed economy, gender discrimination is not a big issue. That with nearly half the workplace already populated by women, we have come a long way from the day the first American woman joined a factory. With so many women CEOs and heads of government departments, do we really need to discuss gender sensitivity any longer? The truth is, while in developing countries sexism is widely prevalent, in developed countries it may not be endemic but still requires a conversation.

In every profession around the world, more women are joining the workforce. In addition to the issue of gender discrimination, professionals need to understand the issue of sexual harassment at work. Consider the case of the head of sales in a leading Indian company with a great professional reputation. He was the ultimate rainmaker. Based out of the company's U.S. office in California, the man felt an attraction to his secretary and, going by her account of the events that followed, used his positional power and influence to have sex with her. After going through the awkward relationship for some time, she left the job. But he began to stalk her. She registered a case, got a restraining order against him and gathered the courage to sue her former employer and the man for sexual harassment. The company made an out-of-court settlement, as did the man, who also "resigned" from his job.

In another instance, a project manager at MindTree started showering extra attention toward a young woman developer. He called her into his office every now and then under the pretext of giving her feedback, but instead would get personal with his questions in one-on-one meetings, make statements about her dress and started sending her romantic text messages. She asked him to stop, but he persisted. She reported the matter to the organization. The text message trail was enough to show that the man had indeed crossed the line. He was a star performer but was asked to leave.

Research in the United States has shown that 95 percent of women have received sexual material such as letters and phone calls at work. In roughly one out of two cases, the sexual harasser is the victim's supervisor; and nine out of ten sexually harassed women suffer from debilitating stress reactions, including depression and headaches. According to Linda Gordon Howard, author of *The Sexual Harassment Handbook*, most ugly situations can be avoided if people follow the three rules our parents taught us whenever we went to the playground early on in life: do not force someone to play, do not be mean and do not pick on little kids. What this conveys is, first, that you must not coerce anyone to have a relationship. Second, you cannot be vindictive if the person rejects your advances. Finally, those who are in positions of power, authority, rank or hierarchy must not prey on a subordinate in the workplace.

Linda Howard rightly points out that not all sexual harassment involves men harassing women. It can be the other way around, as well as between two persons of the same sex. Despite the fact that sexual harassment at work can occur across genders, it is still largely the female worker who is at the receiving end. In a social culture that believes women must be wooed and "pursued," and a "no" is supposed to mean "yes," many of those accused of sexual harassment look perplexed and innocent and claim that they did not know they were doing something wrong in the first place.

Howard also brings forth the need for articulation of an organization's stand and for educating people at work across genders. The crux of the matter lies in an organization's clearly defining what is and is not acceptable behavior. In short, any "unwelcome" gesture is a potential cause for harassment if it persists. Thus whether it emanates from a man to a woman or otherwise, a "no" must always be taken as a "no."

For the professional organization of the future, addressing gender sensitivity and sexual harassment will be very important. Gender sensitivity, however, cannot just be an organizational priority; it is also for every individual to take the initiative to observe, learn, cultivate and demonstrate. Wherever adults work, there is bound to be mutual attraction, but every professional must know where consent stops and harassment begins.

## Chapter 53

# Cross-Cultural Sensitivity

The Lufthansa flight from New York to Frankfurt was delayed by seven hours. When the flight finally landed in Frankfurt, there was chaos. People were tired and anxious. Most had missed their connections to other parts of Europe and Asia. As soon as people deplaned, everyone ran to the nearest customer service representative and there were long lines of passengers wanting to know how they would get rerouted, when their baggage would arrive and a dozen other things. The airline representatives were as harried as the passengers themselves.

Standing in line ahead of me were a young American woman and her friend, fuming like most of the others. In times like these, lines seem endless and the person at the service desk always seems to be taking forever. Finally, the young woman's turn came. The German woman at the service desk asked her, "What's your problem?"

All hell broke loose.

The young American woman screamed, "It's *you* who has a problem. Not me." It was very obvious she was furious at the question. The German woman was taken aback by the passenger's fury and soon enough an angry exchange ensued.

In her own country the American passenger was used to being asked something like, "May I help you?" "What's your problem?" was an affront in the American context. To the German, trained for efficiency, "What's your problem?" was just an expression of interest to immediately engage with the issue at hand and offer a solution. The German was expecting a specific reply, such as that the passenger required hotel accommodation, or needed to make the next connection to Prague or wanted to check the status of her baggage. She did not realize that the direct nature of the question could have a different nuance for the American. The encounter would have been very different if the parties were cross-culturally more aware. Then, before climbing up an emotional ladder, they would first ask, Is there something I might be missing here?

In 1991, when I was working for Wipro, I was in a tight spot with a leading technology organization from Silicon Valley. Doing work offshore was not the norm in those days. As a result, few knew the intricacies involved, far less the impact of culture on globally distributed teams. My client was clearly upset. The work delivered was different from what was agreed upon, they insisted. I drew their attention to the agreement. Then they said that the agreement had been revisited after our technical lead showed them the first prototype; at that time they had told him they now needed many other things included as part of the same specifications. Our technical lead seemed to have agreed with everything during that one meeting, they said. It was my turn to be surprised. I had not been updated about this development.

"But right through the long meeting we had in our office when we asked for all the features, he kept nodding his head," the perplexed American customer told me. Then I realized what must have happened. To the American, a nod means "Yes." To an Indian, a nod simply means, "I am listening."

It took a lot of convincing on both sides for me to contain the damage done, but finally, everyone got a better handle on the impact of cultural differences on such projects. Despite two decades of globally distributed software development since that incident and a lot more knowledge on how to bridge cultural gaps, every day I learn about new ones.

At MindTree, we assess emotional bonding in large, long-playing project teams that invariably consist of our own people and the client's, and they are often from many different parts of the world. Recently, one such high-performing team was seen experiencing difficulties, and a joint off-site meeting among the leaders from both sides was conducted in London. I invited Lu Ellen Schafer, a consultant from California who advises leading-edge companies around the world on team dynamics, to join us as a process observer. With help from her, we realized that apart from the hiccups of a complex software project, there were some significant cross-cultural issues that were affecting perceptions in the minds of leaders from both sides. The Indians on the team were overall very comfortable with their British counterparts but felt that the British "escalated" issues far too often. When this came up, the British team was perplexed. They said they had escalated issues only twice in the course of an entire year. It turned out that while reporting day-to-day issues that remained unresolved for some reason or another, the British frequently copied their e-mails to their other colleagues. To the Indians, who were still working on a solution to a given problem, this amounted to "escalation," and over time, they thought the British were showing them in a poor light by their frequent act of putting on the copy list. The extension to this perception was that the British did not trust us and were unappreciative of the very diligent efforts being made by the team back in India to fix problems. The British were quite taken aback. They believed that they were simply "keeping everyone informed" and not escalating when copying a mail to others.

Lu Ellen Schafer sees lack of cross-cultural sensitivity among professionals as a real issue around the world. In a recent case study, she describes the following situation:

> During a global dinner in Bangalore with his new engineering team, Heinz, a German engineer, complained that he didn't trust Americans. "Really? Why is that?" asked one of the Indians, Ramesh, since he had had mostly positive experiences with American teammates so far. "They pretend they support you, but they don't. They do not tell you the truth," the German replied. Ramesh was startled that Heinz had such negative feelings, but perhaps he was right. Ramesh would listen carefully in this week's meetings to see if he could see what Heinz was talking about.
>
> The next day Heinz laid out his ideas for a possible new feature. Susan, from California, exclaimed, "You rock, Heinz. I love it!" Heinz narrowed his gaze on Susan and said rather assertively, "So you are one hundred percent behind me? You will support the idea of this new feature?" Susan laughed and replied, "Well, I don't know yet. There are a lot of features to consider."

*Heinz shot Ramesh a look as if to say, "Ha! I told you that you cannot trust them." He put his pen down and said, "Okay, just forget it."*

*Ramesh was puzzled. Something was going on but he couldn't quite figure it out. After all, Heinz had just met Susan. How could he distrust her so soon? What she said sounded like a typical American response, full of enthusiasm and encouragement.*

*Ah, then Ramesh got it! Susan's enthusiasm must have been interpreted by Heinz as a commitment to his idea which she then appeared to take back. But Ramesh knew this was not the right understanding. Rather, it was just an American way of acknowledging someone's idea. Ramesh recalled the first few times Americans had said to him, "Great job, Ramesh!" He had loved the compliment, but then realized that Americans usually say "great job" to everyone all the time. Surely not everyone was doing a great job. And then it occurred to him: "Great" in the US had another meaning. It appeared to mean "thank you." He would quietly tell Heinz about this cultural difference the next time they spoke.*

Lu Ellen Schafer tells me that cultural differences are but one of the many factors that affect how people respond to various situations. Such differences seem to matter most when things are not going well. When professionals are communicating openly, when a project is on track and the deadlines are reasonable, most cultural differences are noted as interesting, if they are noted at all. However, when distance, time zone differences, overly aggressive deadlines, highly stressed clients or unclear roles and responsibilities create tension, cultural differences can exacerbate the apprehension on both sides.

Just because most of us speak English does not mean we understand one another while doing business around the world. In an increasingly global world, we have to learn cross-cultural nuances because we deal with customers, suppliers and other collaborators who are as new to us as we are to them. A professional who understands these differences and finds ways to work with them, rather than letting them work against the organization, will be in much demand in the new world.

# Chapter 54

# Governance

Let me tell you the story of the time MindTree went public and what happened to the career of an exceptionally bright young man. A public listing is the perfect occasion to say thank you to employees of a company through an assured allocation of stocks that is permissible under the law. However, such allocation comes with a lock-in because stock exchange regulations do not allow employees to sell (dump) their shares in the market and make quick money the moment the share price goes up. The reason is simple. While only a few retail shareholders may get an allocation in an oversubscribed public issue, an employee who gets an assured allocation is already getting preferential treatment, and the law requires that such a person return the favor by holding on to the stock and not making short-term gains at the cost of a retail investor. Hence the mandatory lock-in period. Hundreds of MindTree employees benefited under the scheme and were bound by the lock-in period of a year. The young man in question took a large bank loan and purchased shares from the special employee quota. The moment the stock listed and its value went up within days, the employee off-loaded his shares. He thought that in the thousands of transactions performed every day, nobody would notice. The problem for people who contravene the law today is that digital footprints are easy to track. As soon as the matter surfaced, the individual was asked to leave and the stock exchange was notified, for he had broken insider trading rules that employees of every listed company must abide by. It was a clear breach of governance.

In the days to come, the term "governance" will touch professionals in every field in one way or another. Broadly, it is a word that encompasses compliance with the laws of the land but in spirit asks for self-regulation. If you think about it, a company, or any organization for that matter, is not a living thing and is quite incapable of breaking laws. Thus when institutions break laws, it is actually someone working there who has broken the law.

Basic governance issues could arise in numerous situations, as when purchasing goods and services for personal use from vendors to your company or when selecting vendors and awarding contracts. Paying money or other forms of inducement to get your work done is a clear breach of governance.

If you are the purchase manager and if one of the bidders is even distantly related to you, you need to step out of the process voluntarily. If you do not, that is a governance issue.

If you are the head of finance and your brother-in-law is the banker you deal with but you fail to disclose that relationship to your organization, that is a governance issue.

A doctor, a lawyer or a chartered accountant who has advisory capacity cannot take advantage of his position with a client to secure preferential benefits.

This is not a book on governance. The intent here is to take the first steps in sensitizing professionals. They must hereafter actively seek information and guidance on this issue when they are members of any given profession.

Most governance issues can be avoided with a culture of education and a spirit of full disclosure. When there is the slightest possibility of a conflict of interest, prenotify the relationships. Dr. Sridhar Mitta, a pioneer of the Indian IT industry, had a nice way of explaining how to avoid problematic situations in governance that sometimes arise out of the seemingly innocent acts of a professional. "Never drink milk under a palm tree," he would say. For the uninitiated, a palm tree is a source of toddy, an alcoholic beverage of great potency. If I were seen drinking under it, even if it was lemonade and not the real thing, the conclusion people would make is going to be very obvious. Thus it is important to be careful about perceptions we create. The point here is that we must be doing not only the right thing or staying away from the wrong, but we must also be aware of perceptions sometimes created with unintended but avoidable acts

As businesses become global and more complex, there will be an increasing demand for governance that meets requirements across countries. How do you self-regulate to ensure that you do not break the laws laid down by different governments? Is it something that only organizations need to worry about? Or is it something every employee of an organization, or for that matter every self-employed professional, needs to understand?

Chapter 55

# Intellectual Property

When he joined MindTree, he looked infallible in every respect. He was an outstanding technologist who would do any organization proud with his great ability to build embedded applications on semiconductor chips. But after joining us, he built an application for a MindTree customer in which he reused portions of software that he had previously written while in the employ of an earlier organization. When the issue surfaced, he claimed innocence. He had no idea he had created a legal exposure for himself as well as for MindTree. The man did not know that the software he had designed while in the pay of his earlier employer was what we call "work for hire" and the rights did not belong to him. Worse, his bringing out that code when moving to MindTree was itself an illegal act. If by chance the code had gone unnoticed and the ownership issue surfaced after the chip went to market, the client for whom we had designed the chip would have been liable as well.

•   •   •

In another organization, a bunch of designers created a prototype of a piece of equipment and got the customer's approval for the project. When the actual design was in progress, it turned out that the prototype contained what is called "open source software." The problem with using certain kinds of open source software is that by virtue of its being available free, if you build an application based on it, that application may not enjoy any trade protection. For a customer, it is of no use to buy a design that starts off with no competitive advantage because the design has been created in part from open source code. When this fact surfaced, the customer asked the team to rewrite the entire code, and then all hell broke loose. It was only then that the team realized it was a Herculean task and that they did not quite understand the logic and algorithm behind the components taken from the open source software. Though they might have the capability to figure it out, the timeline for doing so was going to be very different from the original understanding with the customer. It became a reverse engineering nightmare that could have been avoided if engineers knew the basics of governance.

An advertising agency showed a prototype Web site design to a client. The client loved it. The Web site went live. After many months, a U.S.-based company that sells stock photographs sued the client because the Web site had used stock shots downloaded from its site. When the client asked the Web site designer, he washed his hands of the issue. He simply drew attention to the fine print in his agreement that required the client to get the necessary approvals for any visual/graphics that might be used. But it was the moral responsibility of the Web site designer to draw specific attention, based on that clause, to the source of the photo-graphs he was using and to clearly inform the advertising agency that the rights to use those photographs had to be obtained from the source before using them. And it was negligence on the part of the advertising agency not to pay attention to this clause in the contract which exposed them and their client to the possibility of being sued.

What was the issue the employees above failed to grasp? That using someone else's creative work comes with the responsibility to seek prior permission; it comes with the requirement that it is duly acknowledged and, where necessary, paid for. And if the work was done while in the employ of another organization, you do not have the right to use it in your current organization: it does not belong to you, unless otherwise stated in writing.

You could be a doctor, engineer, graphic designer, architect, teacher or musician. The new world requires every professional to understand the basics of intellectual property rights. In the old world, we had little everyday interaction and exposure to such concepts. It was okay if we broadly understood the rights of usage and ownership of immovable and movable property like land, building, machinery or cattle. But today, with more value get-ting generated by the use of knowledge, it is every professional's responsibility to acquire a basic understanding of concepts like copyright, patents and trademarks. And it is every professional's responsibility not to expose an organization or a client to lawsuits that could result from negligence in this area.

Chapter 56

# Sustainability

There was a time when I used to agitate a lot about the overflowing dustbins in the neighborhood I live in. I could not stand the apathy of people who simply threw the garbage around and not inside the dustbin. On weekends, I would routinely pick up the garbage strewn around the bins and put it all inside.

This taught me valuable lessons about my own limitations. But it also taught me that the biggest culprits for creating non-biodegradable material are consumer goods companies, those that use shampoo sachets, food wrappers, plastic tubes and containers, and those that make diapers and all other forms of material that will sit in a landfill for the next thousand years and release toxins into the soil and air. This includes the thin plastic bags all of us pick up at the grocery or convenience store. In the developing countries of the world, even before they go to the landfill, municipal workers simply take such garbage and set fire to it just outside the town limits, releasing poisonous gases into the atmosphere.

In almost all consumer products companies, most of them

multinationals, the people in charge are qualified management professionals, and while they may choose to ignore the environmental consequences of their products today, tomorrow is another story. Professionals will have to know how their work could potentially destroy the earth and, conversely, how they can help sustain it.

Today, we think that only corporations and the government have to worry about issues like global warming and carbon footprint. The truth is that every profession and as a result every professional has a much closer relationship to these issues than we realize.

When a doctor opens a clinic, how does he dispose of medical waste?

An architect suggests a design for a house or an office. What about educating the client on the implications of lighting and air conditioning and ways to save energy?

You open a new campus for your organization. Initially, all you worry about is following local laws that regulate zoning and such things. But now, thousands of people begin to commute to work and when they commute from afar, they add to the carbon footprint. When you pay attention to their transportation needs and look at location options from all angles, you contribute to the process of creating sustainability. In places where thousands of workers eat every day, food waste can create serious health hazards. Wanton use of plastic cups and other such nonbiodegradable items will add to the problems of environmental management. And what about reusing waste paper? How about reducing use of water in toilets, encouraging rainwater harvesting and the use of solar-powered lighting?

You are the buyer of raw material in a food products company. You have to pay attention to the practices of your supply chain. You must apply your mind and understand how much water the farmers consume, what pesticides they are using, how they may be subjecting the earth to chemical torture by excessive use of chemical fertilizer. If you source materials from developing countries, you need to understand the social implications of inducing farmers to move away from cultivating rice and wheat to raising other cash crops. Each of these examples expands the scope of a professional's responsibilities vis-à-vis the environment and the people who are affected by our strategies and actions.

The next time you buy coffee at Starbucks, pay attention to the paper coffee cup. It says Starbucks buys beans from growers who abide by standards laid down by the Rainforest Alliance. Starbucks does so because it clearly matters to Starbucks customers what sustainability measures the company follows. In March 2007 the *Financial Times* reported, "As big global companies address sustainability, many are focusing on agricultural water use. Companies such as Nestlé, Starbucks and Kraft have recognized the need to address water conservation in supply chains. To do so, Kraft and Chiquita have turned to the Rainforest Alliance, a non-profit conservation organization that monitors the sustainability of agricultural producers."

Sustainability is no longer a "peacenik" fad. Issues like potable water, waste disposal, greenhouse gases and carbon emissions can be directly linked to every profession, and more significantly to how every professional makes a living.

But even before people take responsibility for the larger cause, the first step is to get educated on the basics of sustainability and become aware of all subsequent individual actions. Professionals in the new world will need to develop a personal context for the phrase "doing well by doing good." Because tomorrow's customers will seek out those who are proactive in their practices to make the planet a better place to live in.

Part Seven

# The Professional's Professional

Chapter 57

# A Yen for Professionalism

One of the countries I deeply admire for its professionalism is Japan. I have visited Japan many times but learned about the Japanese people closely during my training in TQM in 1996. Japan has become what it is today due in some part to its great corporations and the people behind them.

I tasted the professionalism of the country the very first time I visited. The taxi driver who was to take me to my hotel did not know the shortest route (these were the days before navigation systems in cars). Though he brought me almost to the road on which the hotel was located, he took a wrong turn, and as a result of the one-way system, had to go around a couple of blocks before arriving at my destination. I did not mind because I was not in a hurry and it wasn't his fault at all. But when I paid him the metered fare, the driver returned some money. I was very surprised and after a labored conversation—the driver did not know English and I did not understand Japanese—I realized that he was refunding the money for the last leg of the trip when he had gone around a couple of blocks. It was his job to know the route and he could not charge me for what he felt was his mistake!

The second immediate lesson was waiting for me as soon as I entered the hotel. I was still recovering from the shock of the taxi driver's honesty. The porter from the hotel brought in my suitcase. I offered him a tip. The man went red in the face. He backed off a few steps and kept mumbling, "No, sir, no tip. This is Japan."

During subsequent years as an occasional visitor to Japan, I learned how the idea of professionalism permeates the nation and to what lengths Japanese go to live the idea. Professionalism in Japan blends with three other things: national pride, precedence of the group over the individual and, finally, the spiritual identity of the culture.

Years after my visits to Japan, I was exchanging notes on professionalism with Infosys chairman Narayana Murthy and he told me the story about the time he visited the Japanese department store Matsuzakaya, which has a ten-story outlet in the Ginza district of Tokyo. Murthy was being shown around the store by his Japanese host. As the two got out of an elevator, a young Japanese woman in a kimono welcomed them with a smile and ushered them in, as is customary at Matsuzakaya. Murthy blurted out in English that this must be a boring job. His host immediately translated what he had said. The girl listened attentively, smiled, bowed and replied in Japanese, which was dutifully interpreted by the host. She said, "I have been paid by my company to make my customers feel welcome. I try hard to do a good job. And I am very proud of it."

Years after the incident, Murthy still shrinks with embarrassment at what he calls his "silly, thoughtless remark."

• • •

A Japanese passerby stopped to watch a monk at work. He was picking up dry twigs from a garden patiently, dutifully, one by one, the whole day. The man finally asked, "O Holy One, when will your work stop?" The monk replied, without looking up, "When the last dry twig has been removed."

To the Japanese, work is a living experience. How can we all try to improve things around us? Where does the human endeavor to be a better professional stop? In the garden of work, as long as the garden is alive, there is no last dry twig.

I stated at the beginning of this book that I have drawn on the experience of many men and women whom I have met in the course of my work over the years and whom I consider to be benchmarks of professionalism in their respective fields. They come from various backgrounds: banker, lawyer, advertising head, salesperson, software developer, program manager, doctor, journalist, accountant, photographer. I asked these eminent men and women what qualities they admired in a professional and what they considered unprofessional conduct. I collated all their feedback to rank the top ten attributes of a professional:

1. Integrity
2. Commitment and ownership
3. Action orientation and goal seeking
4. Continuous learning
5. Professional knowledge/skills
6. Communication

7.  Planning, organizing and punctuality
8.  Quality of work
9.  A positive attitude, approachability, responsiveness
10. Being an inspiring reference to others

It is heartening that integrity came out right on top, and that is how this book opens, with an expansive discussion on a subject that is often considered prudish but in reality is the keystone of the arch. Commitment and ownership come second. What is interesting to note is that action orientation precedes continuous learning. I believe this implies that sometimes it is learning on the job that saves the day and that requires agility and networking. We live in an age of just-in-time learning. So it is not about how much you already know but about how rapidly you can tap in to other experts and utilize their help and their knowledge required to solve a problem. And that requires commitment, ownership and action orientation. Planning, organizing, punctuality and quality of work have to be delivered with a great attitude; otherwise a client will in all probability not like to do business with you a second time.

But the last attribute really opened up my eyes: being an inspiring reference to others. Tomorrow's professional must have a beaconlike presence in a world that will ask for memorability. Because being ordinary will no longer be considered professional.

# Chapter 58

# The Unprofessional

The preceding pages have discussed what it means to be a professional, how one can become a better professional and what it will take to be a professional in the twenty-first century. Unfortunately, the discussion would not be complete without mentioning how equally important it is for any professional to be aware of unprofessional conduct, because sometimes it is very easy to slip into this behavior without realizing it.

Here are my top ten markers of unprofessional conduct:

## 1. Missing a Deadline

It happens to all of us all the time. You are waiting for a flight and it is well past the scheduled boarding time. No announcement has been made, and no one has told you the reason for the delay or the rescheduled departure time. Or you go to the laundry to collect your clothes and find that your clothes are not ready. You call your advertising agency and they say they are not ready with the presentation scheduled for this afternoon.

You are waiting for a software release that was to happen over the weekend. It is already Monday afternoon; there is no sign of it.

We have all been victims of missed deadlines, but when it comes to us, we all too quickly forget that we may be doing it to others as well.

## 2. Failing to Be Forthright

Behind the unprofessional conduct of missing deadlines is often poor estimation of the time required to get the job done. Sometimes missing a deadline is due to unavoidable circumstances. The thing to do in either case is to bring the bad news up ahead of time and tell the other person that you are going to miss the deadline—but do it well before the deadline, not after it.

There is always some problem or other that has come in the way of meeting the deadline. But we all know that most problems announce their arrival in advance. But someone, somewhere, pretends that a problem does not exist or, if ignored, it will solve itself. And then it all just blows up.

If communicated proactively to the right person, most problems not only get addressed, but they can be converted into an opportunity.

If it is really bad news, try to deliver it in person. At the very least call personally. No e-mails. No carefully left voice mails at the customer's office past midnight knowing that no one will pick up the phone at that hour. Call the number most likely to be picked up in two rings and tell it like it is. Better still, show up in person.

We do not communicate problems due to fear of reprisal, rejection and sometimes loss of business. The price for such denial can be very heavy in the organizational context.

Noncommunication remains one of the top reasons why things go wrong in delivering products and services to people who depend on us.

## 3. Withholding Information

A professional is privy to special information by virtue of his or her professional relationship. It is a relationship of trust. A doctor, a lawyer, a counselor may have access to a person's private life. Such people have to notify the recipient of their service of all conflicting interests they may have, and all such disclosure must happen in a proactive manner. Withholding such information is a malafide act.

## 4. Not Respecting Privacy of Information

Similarly, information received in the course of a professional relationship must be held in confidence, and if it is likely to be remotely confidential or proprietary, it can be parted with only after explicit consent of the other party. Consent should never be assumed. However close and long-standing the relationship may be, consent has to be formally sought and formally recorded each time there is a transaction.

Sometime ago my daughter sent me an e-mail, forwarding a rather excited communication from a friend of hers. This individual, who works for an international bank, had written to her that I had just opened an account with them. MindTree had decided to

shift its payroll from one bank to another and that required everyone to open a salary account with the new bank. I was taken aback
by the indiscretion of the young man. While the intent may have
been innocent, it is unacceptable professional conduct. I do not
want my lawyer, my doctor or my banker to go around talking
about my business with them to other people.

As businesses become part of the global mainstream, one of
the things all professionals will have to understand is the importance of privacy. In some parts of the world, people are not used
to privacy. However, that is not how the world works. As a result,
every professional, irrespective of the field of work, must understand the inviolability of a client's information privacy.

## 5. Not Respecting "Need to Know"

There are an increasing number of spouses who work. Sometimes, they may even work in the same organization. When they
do so, it is important to avoid what is known as "pillow talk"—
sharing official information at home. The first test one must use
for this is: But for the marital relationship, would the other person
have access to a particular piece of information? And second, does
the spouse pass the "need to know" test?

## 6. Plagiarizing

You cannot pass off as your own what does not belong to you.
While taking from someone's ideas and most certainly while
quoting from someone's work, a professional must acknowledge
the source. Too many people—students, teachers, researchers—

routinely pass off as original work that clearly does not belong to them.

In today's world, there is enough technology to track down piracy and plagiarism, whether in text, in graphics or in any other form. Every professional knows that resources like Google and Wikipedia are universally available. Given the pressures of time to create an impressive presentation, it is easy to succumb to the temptation to "research" the net, download charts and graphs and simply embed them in a slide deck or a report.

A professional must do three things when depending on such sources: state why you have chosen to pull out a specific set of information, acknowledge the source and, most important, state your own reasoned conclusion. A professional must state her point of view, not pass off someone else's as if it were her own.

## 7. Passing the Blame

When things go wrong, many people fault their subordinate, executive assistant or student researcher. Passing along the blame is an unprofessional thing to do. When a doctor, an engineer, a lawyer or an architect blames his or her people in front of a client, it reflects poorly on the professional's own caliber. The last thing you should be doing is separating yourself from your junior's or assistant's inadequacies. It goes against the grain of inclusion and ownership. Just as we say a poor workman blames his tools, a bad professional blames his associates.

## 8. Overstating Qualifications and Experience

Unfortunately, job seekers sometimes trivialize the difference between exposure and expertise when it comes to writing résumés. Those who know about something only at a superficial level often write about it in their résumés as if they have mastery over the subject.

No one individual can be great at everything. There is no need to embellish one's capabilities while applying for a job. I have often received résumés of young engineers who have done just an internship of short duration in an organization, but who claimed to have designed an entire enterprise application while being there. In many parts of the world, you are taken at face value. If you say that you know something or have done something, it is not contested. So while it may be easy to bluff one's way into a job or an assignment, it becomes a complete loss of face at the time of execution and leaves a bad taste in everyone's mouth.

## 9. Frequently Changing Jobs

Close to the malaise of overstated qualifications is that of mindless job changes. In every interview with frequent job-hoppers, the conversation is very predictable. It is either a story of "I was okay, my organization was not," or "I was not looking for a change, I got head-hunted." If someone has had five such changes in a ten-year career, it is unlikely that you are looking at an "organization man"; you are probably looking at a competent mercenary. As one progresses professionally, one must understand that failed job changes have as much to do with the individual as with the organization, and that people who pass off the blame simply demonstrate an opportunistic mind-set.

## 10. Not Taking Care of Your Appearance

Finally, professional conduct has to do with professional appearance and personal hygiene. It is not just for a doctor, a police officer or a pilot to be properly attired, nor is it only about wearing a uniform. Every profession has its own acceptable dress code that may sometimes be written and sometimes not. When it is not, and just because sometimes your organization does not emphasize it, that does not mean you can take liberties with it.

Your attire must inspire credibility, and whether you are a man or a woman, dressing in a way that distracts is not a great idea, be it flashy ornaments or a dress with a deep neckline.

# Chapter 59

# Return of the Dead

On March 31, 2009, Bangalore woke up to this headline on the front page of *The Times of India*:

*4 cops sell unclaimed body, get booted out*

According to the paper, sometime in August 2006, the police station in Madivala, a Bangalore locality, got a call from a hotel owner. The man reported a dead body lying outside his hotel. The policemen picked up the dead body and declared that it was a case of death of a mentally retarded man who had fallen on thorns. They subsequently took the body to a medical college as unclaimed and sold the dead man. Medical colleges buy dead bodies for teaching purposes.

When the dead man's son surfaced and lodged a complaint about his missing father, one thing led to another, and finally the whole story came out.

After the investigations, the police commissioner dismissed an inspector, a subinspector, an assistant subinspector and a constable for their complicity in this shocking case.

These policemen, despite their professional training, their uniform, their power and their authority, can never be considered professionals.

In sharp contrast, Mahadeva, the man whose profession is the burial of unclaimed dead bodies, a man who arrived with no means, possessed no education and did not have organizational mentorship, will always remain a professional's professional.

Because, ultimately, being a professional is a matter of personal choice and the values we opt to live by.

# Chapter 60

# Platform and Purpose

Your profession is a platform. It is something of a springboard; a place from which you start a journey on the road to someplace else. Your purpose, on the other hand, determines how far you may go on that journey, for whom it is undertaken and how meaningful it is.

When thinking about the relationship between your platform and purpose, imagine a two-by-two matrix in which our existence is defined by the $x$ coordinate that represents the platform and the $y$ coordinate that represents the purpose. Between these two, there are four quadrants. We predominantly live in one of the four.

There are some whose existence can be called "low platform and low purpose." There are those who would fit into "high platform and low purpose." Then there are some who live a life best described as "low platform and high purpose." Only a very few go on to lead a life that can be described as "high platform and high purpose." All four options are available in equal measure as we start life, but as life progresses, as professionals we tend to settle into one or the other. Let us examine each one briefly.

## Low Platform and Low Purpose

Imagine an ordinary but good-natured high school student who decides to attend a community college even as his classmates go on to the most competitive schools in the country. He earns an ordinary college degree along the way and upon graduating settles down in the family business. He has a small family, builds a reasonable dwelling and remains in relative anonymity.

In the years ahead, he takes care of his immediate needs; he does not venture beyond the familiar and has no ambition to change the world.

Similarly but somewhat differently, some of us, despite stellar professional qualifications, also settle into a comparable life, content with the on-the-job training, the allocated work, the predictable good salary, the postings and assignments that come along the way. These folks stay close to the median and after a few decades of work, of raising a family, simply fade into oblivion. Theirs is a low-platform and low-purpose life. People who stay here are the vast majority that make the world a predictable, often dependable place in which to live, but they leave no lasting impact.

This life is okay as long as you are comfortable with its consequences and make no false comparison with others. Chances are, you will live a life of contentment, and while you do not leave behind a mark, you also do not make things difficult for people around you.

The redeeming aspect of being low platform and low purpose

is that people in this quadrant do not consume resources dispro-portionate to the impact they make; they take from life what is minimally needed; they are not overly materialistic and do not amass wealth and fortune at other people's cost. They have a lower carbon footprint in every sense. These are people who are driven by the sheer need to exist. Existence is the driver of their being.

## High Platform and Low Purpose

The people who live in this quadrant are usually highly qualified and highly competent, but they lead a self-serving life. They are predominantly concerned with what others have that they do not have. They use their education, experience and contacts to see how best to get ahead in life. Both material acquisition and orga-nizational power are very critical to them, as is social recognition. To them, platform is everything. They are very unlikely to risk it because it largely defines their existence. These are people who are more likely to pursue the predictable.

Consider some of the people you know in your own profes-sional circle who fit into this quadrant. As I said, they are bright and intelligent and they probably planned their entire lives early on in their existence. That life script consisted of first landing a good job, then getting a master's degree or an MBA at a brand-name school after a couple of years, then a global assignment. They married equally covetable, equally qualified spouses and fo-cused on building a high-net-worth life from the very start. These people are often in positions of leadership and they are seldom aware that they are leading a life of high platform and low pur-pose. They genuinely believe that they are hugely beneficial to life and living. They do not think there could be anything more significant than professional ambition. Aggressive pursuit of their personal goals determines their choice of work and their employer, whose brand value brings them critical social recognition. Such people are well suited to handle a large company assignment, but they are not cut out to start something on their own. They depend on a given organizational path for personal success, but they do not create their own path.

People in this quadrant believe that their biggest contribution to society is their own life. For the most part, they think they are indispensable. But, then, they are also the easiest to replace because for everyone who leaves, there is a long waiting list to get into their shoes. The driver of their existence is consumption.

## Low Platform and High Purpose

In the lower extreme quadrant is a handful that decides somewhat early on in life that the rat race of the high-platform, low-purpose life is not what they are cut out for.

These are people who become start-up entrepreneurs. Some are also idealistic individuals who want to make a difference to society in ways other than building a business. They do not believe that institutions like the government and the established large organizations, particularly those in the private sector, have the capacity or the sensitivity to make a difference. They decide, not out of compulsion but out of choice, that they must make a direct personal impact, however small, to a cause dear to them.

There are some real and inherent challenges in being in this quadrant beyond the fact that it entails personal hardship and a minimalist lifestyle. Though the cause may be noble or an entrepreneurial idea may be enticing, working outside an established organizational framework often makes it difficult to succeed.

Professionals in this quadrant need to get their spirit up every morning against all external odds and sustain their souls with none of the rewards or recognition mechanisms that are so readily available to those in the high-platform, low-purpose quadrant. It is often a lonely trek, without any validation that their work is making a tangible difference. That said, those who opt to be in this quadrant do what they do because of who they are. They do not seek instant gratification; they are patient with the change-making process.

But being low platform, their work usually affects some people but does not by itself become scalable. Many things in the world require scale.

The driving force behind people who are low platform and high purpose is path making. Sometimes it is altruistic; sometimes it is driven by a desire to simply own one's destiny.

As we all know, many who begin and sometimes even flounder in this quadrant actually make it to the next one: the one I call high platform and high purpose.

## High Platform and High Purpose

Many professionally qualified people start off on a high platform by virtue of their privileged upbringing. For those who did not come from an elevated socioeconomic background, the academic credential from an institution of repute often provides them a high platform. Thus thousands of professionally qualified people actually start off in life from a high platform compared with millions of others in this world. Their academic achievement, at least temporarily, propels them upward in life. That said, whether or not they are able to retain and build on the high platform actually gets determined by many factors and certainly is not a matter of lifelong entitlement.

Many people make wrong career choices; life is a snakes and ladders game. Sometimes people get lazy along the way. And then there are also the unpredictable circumstances that may rob some of their platform or slide them down to a lower one. But assuming that life deals most of us a reasonable hand, the larger question is whether or not we build high purpose on the high platform that has been provided to us.

When one embraces a high purpose staged from a high platform, one makes the greatest difference to the world.

This is the quadrant of professionals like Steve Jobs, Bill Gates, Warren Buffett, Indra Nooyi, Meg Whitman and Arthur Ashe. Sometimes this class of professionals actually starts in the immediate lower quadrant of low platform and high purpose.

Bill Gates started life designing a BASIC language compiler for an obscure machine called the Altair. Steve Jobs was a geeky youngster who wanted to build a personal computer with great calligraphy. Dr. Govindappa Venkataswamy of Aravind Hospital was just another ophthalmologist, and Narayana Murthy started Infosys with a loan of ten thousand rupees—at the time probably equivalent to US $500—from his wife Sudha.

Somewhere along their respective journeys, these professionals received their call, as we all do at some stage or other. The difference is, when the call comes, most of us may not hear it. Among other things, obsessive love for a platform invariably reduces the power of hearing.

So when the call comes, we must make sure we pick up. The trick is to recognize it and to embrace the cause that it conveys. Destiny does not leave a voice message.

Once a professional embraces the cause, she must cease her love for the platform even as she recognizes its power, because from now on she has to externalize its benefits and look at herself as a lifelong custodian, and not the owner, of the platform.

The people with the ability to make the greatest impact see their professional qualifications, experience and accomplishments as a platform to make a difference to the world; it is not something that they own for their personal glory and greatness.

These are people who have the power of vision and they do three things right: They create a vision community to carry people along and make them feel it is a shared vision. Then they give their entire life to the cause it entails and understand that in the top right-hand quadrant, there is the least scope for instant gratification. Finally, they remain steadfast even in the wake of great personal sacrifices and they do not yield to distractions. They do not let adulation get in the way of their work; nor do they fight battles that take them away from their main purpose. For people in the high-platform, high-purpose quadrant, the size of their vision is larger than life; this is where comfort with scale really matters.

Lofty as it may sound, this quadrant often tests the aspirant with highly dangerous situations that leave no margin of error. One mistake and you drop into the left or the bottom quadrants. People around you are so busy showering their admiration and sometimes plain sycophancy on you that they will not be the ones to hold the mirror up to your face. History is full of examples of high achievers whose fall from their pedestal was rapid and irreversible.

The driving force of people in this quadrant is the desire to leave a legacy.

As we grow up as professionals, all the four options are available to most of us. There is nothing right or wrong about being in any of the four quadrants. The only opportunity for error is to not know which one you are in. Education and experience give us the power to make informed choices, and we need to choose where we want to be and at the same time understand the consequences.

Life is about making choices and not simply succumbing to inevitability.

Life constantly tests our resolve and sometimes rotates us from one quadrant to another to see what conviction we carry in fulfillment of our purpose. As we journey into life, we must continue to strengthen our platform. But we must also remind ourselves that it is only meant to help us catch the train; it is not a place to live.

A true professional knows that through his profession he has the power to make a huge difference to the world around him; he has an uplifting purpose that takes him beyond earning a living to making a difference in life.

# Acknowledgments

*The Professional* is the third in a series of books Portfolio / Penguin and I have done together. During the course of the first two, the idea for this book was conceived with my erstwhile editor, Sumitra Srinivasan. Our free-ranging discussions seemed to bring us back to the questions: Am I a true professional? What qualities would make me a better professional? What is professional ethics? What does it mean for me? Faced with a difficult decision and multiple options, how do I know I am making the right choice? We realized that most people ask themselves these same questions, undergoing moments of uncertainty about how they can be the best. Why not write a book, she kept suggesting, for the scores of people who become doctors, engineers, journalists, architects, teachers—in fact anyone who works in a professional capacity—which they can use to help them guide their decisions and actions? I am grateful to Sumitra for the conversation, her subsequent encouragement, critiques and patience.

When the book appeared in print in India, it became an instant bestseller and was subsequently chosen by Portfolio / Penguin as a candidate for international release. This time, I got the opportunity to work with my present editor, Brooke Carey. While Sumitra is an outstanding ideator, in Brooke I met the quintessential editor. She helped make the book relevant for a global audience. In the process, she also suggested valuable additions and some even more valuable deletions. I have been extremely fortunate to have the guidance of Sumitra and Brooke, in the sequence in which they appeared. I am very grateful to both. Thanks also to Michael Burke, who did a superb copyediting job.

Writing, at one level, is a solitary experience. Had it not been for my life partner of three decades, Susmita, I would not have been able to take on the task of being a writer. She feeds my body and my soul and puts up with the emotional highs and lows that a writer must suffer before he is able to produce anything of meaning. I remain eternally grateful to her for many reasons; one among them is helping me bring this book to you.

As I began writing, I was fortunate to meet Prashanth, an unusually gifted young man, from the Spastics Society of Karnataka. He agreed to be my research assistant for this project—verifying sources, seeking information that may be useful, and questioning the prose and sometimes the purpose. Despite being severely affected by his congenital affliction of cerebral palsy, he provided a tremendous amount of help and symbolizes the spirit of a professional. I thank him for his dedication and enthusiasm, without which this work of love would not have been complete.

At MindTree, my colleague Shanti Uday has been running my life with the patience of a quiet, ever-flowing river for a decade now. Her support has been enormous in helping me with versions, backups and the final editing. I remain always grateful to her. Shanti, thank you for everything.

Working for MindTree has many rewards—chief among them

is the space it provides me to be myself. And the resources to write three books within a span of five years!

As I look back on my working career to find examples of professionalism, I realize how greatly I have been influenced by countless people—bosses, peers and subordinates—from whom I have gleaned lessons in professional behavior. To each one of those individuals I remain indebted. Many lessons from some very special people, whom I call "professional's professionals," are included in this book. These are people to whom I reached out to tell me what they think are the attributes of a professional through personal anecdotes, illustrating both professional and unprofessional conduct. A big thank you to Ashok Soota, Anjan Lahiri, Abhi Dhar, Amit Varma, Asha Mathen, Ashutosh Shukla, Bobby Mitra, Dr. Thimmappa Hegde, Kush Desai, K. Ramesh, Lubna Kably, Lu Ellen Schafer, Mahesh Bhat, Manoj Chandran, Maya Chandra, Mukul Pandya, Milind Sathe, Neelesh Prabhu, Olivier Poulard, Pradipt Kapoor, Raj Rawal, Rajesh Nair, Sudhir K. Reddy, Scott Staples, Suresh Gurumurthy, Tridip Saha, Venkatesh Komarla, Rostow Ravanan and Warren Leudecker. I would fail in my duty if I did not make a special mention of two great people: Mukul Pandya, who helped me with the story of Curtis Perrin, and Professor Vijay Govindarajan for his contributions to chapter 44.

And, finally, dear reader, thank you for buying this book.